EXTRACURRICULARS

Teaching Christianly Outside Class

Robert H. Gundry

WIPF & STOCK · Eugene, Oregon

Wipf and Stock Publishers
199 W 8th Ave, Suite 3
Eugene, OR 97401

Extracurriculars
Teaching Christianly Outside Class
By Gundry, Robert H.
Copyright©2012 by Gundry, Robert H.
ISBN 13: 978-1-62564-577-7
Publication date 1/8/2014
Previously published by Blurb, 2012

Contents

Foreword

Teachers talk a lot in the classroom, but during my thirty-eight years of teaching in the Department of Religious Studies at Westmont College, an evangelically Christian institution located in Santa Barbara, California, I also delivered numerous talks outside the classroom. The present volume contains a selection of those extracurricular talks. Because their occasions differed, each talk is prefaced with a brief identification of its occasion. Topics vary, but the talks have wide-ranging relevance and application. Coming first are those of a scholastic bent. Next come the sermonic, then the controversial, and finally the valedictory. The scholastic were delivered at convocations and as special lectures; the sermonic in chapel services; the controversial in seminars; and the valedictory at baccalaureates and other occasions of farewell. The content of "Diversity in New Testament Christology" is used by permission of Wipf and Stock Publishers. May these talks bring pleasure and profit to a broad audience.

Robert H. Gundry

My thanks to my granddaughter, Madeleine Rose Tappy, for her work in formatting this volume.

Introduction:
Christus Primatum Tenens

~ Delivered in chapel at Homecoming 2012 ~

Back in the fall of 1980, a young man named Gayle Beebe took a class of mine on New Testament theology. Naturally, I gave student Beebe assignments to do; and, I must say, he did them admirably well. But on the present occasion of our celebrating the 75th anniversary of the founding of Westmont College, President Beebe, as he now is, has turned the tables by giving me an assignment. It's to speak to you this morning about Westmont's motto. The motto is inscribed in Latin at the bottom of the college seal: *Christus primatum tenens.*

Tenens: that means "holding." It's the basis of the word "tenant" in English. You're the tenant of a house if by occupying it you hold it. A "tenet" is a belief or a doctrine that you hold. You're "tenacious" if you keep holding onto something. *Primatum*: that means preeminence or, more literally, "first place." We're in the season of elections. The primaries were the first elections. But "first" can have to do with rank instead of time. A prima donna is the ranking female singer, for example, the preeminent one. *Christus*: Latin for "Christ," of course. We'll come back to that one.

3

So there you have Westmont's motto: *Christus primatum tenens*. It comes out of the New Testament—in particular, out of the Apostle Paul's letter to the Colossians, chapter 1, verses 15–20. Seventy-five years ago almost all Protestant Christians in the English-speaking world used the King James Version of the Bible. So in a throwback to that era, I'll quote Colossians 1:15–20 out of the King James Version. To make it doubly authentic, I'll quote the passage out of my deceased father's old, well-worn Scofield Reference Bible, an annotated study edition the sales of which were largely responsible for keeping Oxford University Press from going broke during the Great Depression of the 1930s, exactly when Westmont was founded. The passage refers to Jesus Christ:

> Who is the image of the invisible God, the firstborn of every creature: For by him were all things created, that are in heaven, and that are in earth, visible and invisible, whether they be thrones, or dominions, or principalities, or powers: all things were created by him, and for him: And he is before all things, and by him all things consist. And he is the head of the body, the church: who is the beginning, the firstborn from the dead; that in all things he might have the preeminence. For it pleased the Father that in him should all fulness dwell; And, having made peace through the blood of his cross, by him to reconcile all things unto himself; by him, I say, whether they be things in earth, or things in heaven.

(From now on I'll tweak that translation once in a while.)

Christus primatum tenens echoes the last phrase of verse 18: "that he [Christ] might have the preeminence" or, again more literally, "that he might hold first place." But why is our motto in Latin, a dead language? The answer: Because Latin sounds more academic than English, like *cum laude, magna cum laude,* and *summa cum laude* at graduation ceremonies. And a college is nothing if not academic.

It used to be that knowing Latin was just as necessary to academics as knowing how to use the Internet is nowadays. According to the early Laws of Harvard College, for instance, students had to speak Latin when reciting in class. They also had to compose their written work in Latin. And teachers lectured in Latin, as they had been doing for centuries in colleges and universities. As late as the first quarter of the twentieth century, the early 1900s, you had to have had three years of Latin under your belt before you could even get into Harvard. But Harvard was lax. You had to have had four years of Latin to get into Yale, Dartmouth, Brown, Princeton, Williams, Amherst, Johns Hopkins—as well as into women's colleges such as Wellesley, Vassar, Barnard, Mount Holyoke, and others. To enter what is now Columbia University, Alexander Hamilton, a founding father of our country, had to translate the first ten chapters of John's Gospel from the original Greek into Latin.

Talking about Greek, it might surprise you to learn that Westmont used to have a major in the ancient Greek language. It might surprise you even more to learn that in those early years Greek was the most popular major. More students signed up for it than for any other major. At least that's what I was told in all seriousness by a graduate of the college who came to the seminary I was attending at the time.

Be that as it may, and more to the point, the classical wing of the Greek major at Westmont required not only 26 semester units of Greek, but also "at least" 14 semester units of Latin. Never mind the recommendation of a minor in German as well. You'll find these requirements and the recommendation in Westmont's 1941-42 catalog. The phrase "at least" in connection with Latin comes right out of that catalog. So when in 1940 Dr. Wallace Emerson, Westmont's first president and a psychologist—when on the original design of our seal he used Latin for the motto, *Christus primatum tenens*, he was signaling the goal of academic excellence. And he translated the Latin correctly: "Christ holding first place."

But a funny thing happened on the way to the forum. Somewhere along the way the Latin started getting mistranslated: "Holding Christ preeminent." Wrong! "Holding" and "preeminent" aren't wrong. But the relation of "Christ" to "holding" is wrong. To my knowledge, the mistranslation appeared first in a pamphlet very probably dating from the 1950s. Whoever was responsible for the mistranslation, it started pervading Westmont's publications. You could find it everywhere. In recent years, thank goodness, it's been corrected, though you'll still find remnants of the mistranslation here and there.

"Holding Christ preeminent": for that translation the motto should read, *Christum primatum tenens* (*-um* at the end of *Christ*). That would make Christ the object; he's being held. But what we actually have is *Christus* (*-us* at the end), which makes Christ the subject. He's doing the holding. So what's the big deal? you ask. Why the fuss? Isn't this a picayune detail of Latin grammar that's just as deadly and uninteresting as the whole Latin language is dead?

No! There's an important theological point here. The text in Colossians and our motto don't mean that we are holding

Christ preeminent, in first place. Not at all! His preeminence, his firstness, doesn't depend on us. Christ holds first place whether or not we put him first. Of course we should put him first in our lives as individuals, and in our communal life as a college. But he's preeminent, he holds first place, regardless of what we do. Regardless of what we say. Regardless of what we think. The best we can do is to recognize his preeminence, and our motto represents just such a recognition.

This recognition of Christ's preeminence, of his firstness, underlay the founding of Westmont. With God's help it continues to provide the foundation of all that happens here: in your studies, dear students; in your teaching, dear teachers; in your administration, dear administrators; in your work, dear staff; in your deliberations, dear trustees; and in your careers, dear alumni. If our motto ever becomes a dead letter, if we ever lose the recognition of Christ's preeminence, Westmont will suffer its demise as an evangelically Christian college. God forbid! But just as eternal vigilance is the price of liberty, eternal vigilance is also the price of fidelity to our founding, which is another way of saying fidelity to the preeminence of Christ.

Christ has first place. The theme of his firstness runs throughout Colossians 1:15–20. Early in this passage Christ was said to be "the firstborn of all creation." Not the first to be created. That could be the meaning except for the fact that he's said to have created "all things." He's the creator, not a creature. In biblical times a firstborn son got the lion's share of the family inheritance. So "the firstborn" came also to mean, quite simply, "the heir." Christ is heir of the all things he created. They belong to him. They're his property. We're his property.

That's one way he occupies "first place." So whether we are studying, teaching, or manipulating the things he created—visible and invisible things, personal and impersonal—and whatever the angle of our studying, teaching, and manipulating—whether it's artistic, literary, musical, dramatic, scientific, mathematical, psychological, sociological, economic, biological, kinesiological, philosophical, biblical—whatever the angle, let's engage in all our academic pursuits with the reverent recognition that we're dealing with things that belong to Christ, because he created them. They're his.

With that recognition, there's no room for carelessness. There's no room for shoddy work. There's no room for cheating. There's no room for pride in scholastic achievements. We're graciously being allowed to deal with somebody else's property: Christ's. "Firstborn of all creation," "heir of all creation," "first place."

Here's another way Christ holds first place. It's easy to miss. I'm referring to the statement in verse 17, "and he is before all things." You wouldn't know it in English, but the word translated "before" is actually a prepositional form of the word for "first." In relation to his creation, then, Christ has first place, and always has had it, because he's eternal. He preexisted the all things he created. He's first in time as well as first in rank.

So as somebody famously said, we think our Creator's thoughts after him. When we think truly about the earth, sea, and sky, the sun, moon, and stars, about plant and animal life, about human nature, human history, human industry—when in our reading and experimenting and artistry we think christianly about all these objects of study that make up our college curriculum, we are thinking the thoughts of Christ, who before he created those objects, thought about them, because he is, was, and always has been "before all things." First!

What an astounding, exciting privilege to be thinking his thoughts after him! To be delving into his mind! Do you really appreciate how wonderful this privilege is? Make the most of it! Don't let it be said of you, students—don't let it be said of you that education is wasted on the young. To honor Christ, prove that saying wrong, because out of his creative mind he formed the very subject matter of all the arts and sciences. You are following his lead.

First in rank. First in time. And now, first in resurrection. This is the third way Christ holds first place. Verse 18: he is "the firstborn from among the dead," that is, the first to be resurrected. Not a temporary resuscitation in his case, but a permanent resurrection. Here "firstborn" does have its temporal meaning; and the result, the accomplished purpose, of his resurrection, Paul says, is that particularly in relation to us, his church, Christ himself, and he alone, has come to have first place in all things, in all respects.

More especially, though, because he's first in resurrection, our own resurrection as people who belong to him is assured—or, as Paul says in chapter 3, "Your life is hidden with Christ in God. When Christ, who is your life, is revealed, then you too will be revealed with him in glory." A bright future awaits us, a future gloriously bright with resurrection to eternal life.

Finally, Christ holds first place "because [as our text goes on to say] all the fullness [of deity] was pleased to dwell in him"—"bodily," Paul adds in the next chapter of Colossians: the fullness of deity dwelling in Christ not as a myth, not as a dream, not as a thought, not as a fiction; but dwelling in him as a living, breathing, real human being.

9

The fullness of deity was pleased to dwell bodily in Christ. First place indeed!

Let me close with some lines written by the great hymn-writer Charles Wesley. I culled these lines from *An Anthology of Christian Literature*, my most treasured book after the Bible itself.* The anthology was compiled by Dr. Grace Hamilton King, an early teacher of literature here at Westmont whom David Hubbard, one of our most illustrious alumni, once described to me as unforgettably brilliant in the classroom. Later than her time at Westmont, when she was teaching at Glendale City College and I was studying under her husband elsewhere in Los Angeles, she befriended me with a complimentary copy of the anthology. In the form of a prayer addressed to Jesus, the lines she took from Wesley personalize Paul's text and our motto. Here are those lines:

> Jesus, my all in all Thou art,
> My rest in toil, mine ease in pain;
> The med'cine of my broken heart;
> In war, my peace; in loss, my gain;
> . . .
> In want, my plentiful supply;
> In weakness, mine almighty power;
> In bonds, my perfect liberty;
> My light in Satan's darkest hour;
> In grief, my joy unspeakable;
> My life in death; my heaven, my all.

We who believe in Jesus recognize him to be, as he truly is, the one who in all things holds first place. *Christus primatum tenens.*

---

* Now available online at:
   http://www.dickbohrerbooks.com/DownloadFiles/Anthology.pdf

Part One:

Scholastic Talks

College Education as Dessert

~ Delivered at a dessert reception for new students ~

That's the short title. The long title is "An Evangelical Christian Liberal Arts College Education as Dessert." But I thought a title that long would sound more like a full-scale dinner.

So what do I mean by a college education as dessert? What's a dessert in the first place? Well, a dessert is what you deserve, what you deserve for eating such food as potatoes, asparagus, and turnips. Take potatoes, for instance. What a bland, tasteless, dull, unexciting food. And I grew up in Idaho, a state famous for its potatoes. I could never understand why of all the foods in the world they had to pick potatoes as the one food you had to have for every main meal. No matter what else was on the table, there sat the potatoes—always. I got sick of them. Then I heard about the Irish Potato Famine in the 1840s and thought to myself, "What a wonderful time and place to have lived in! No potatoes to eat!"

Then there's asparagus. I know, some people consider it a delicacy. It's expensive. But it's also long and stringy and tastes like cooked grass. My mother used to send me into the apple orchard to pick asparagus. It grew wild there. I hated the job. Worse yet, she cooked what I'd picked and I had to eat it. Not just the tender tips, either. The tough, stringy stalks too. I had to eat what I hated to pick, and I had to pick what I hated to eat. Reminds me of a custom in China: they make you buy the bullet with which you are going to be executed.

But worst of all were the turnips. I couldn't stand their taste. Philosophers talk about the problem of evil: Why is there so much evil in the world? Well, I hadn't seen much evil in the world; but for me, growing up, the problem of evil was, Why did God create turnips?

But eat your potatoes, eat your asparagus, eat your turnips. Then you get dessert. You deserve it! It's your just desert. You've already had your potatoes and turnips and peas and carrots and spinach and broccoli in kindergarten through twelfth grade. You're in college now. It's time for dessert. You got the right GPA, the high SAT. Here's your reward. And those of us who work here aim to make your time with us rewarding. We're serving you dessert.

Now dessert time is a time of leisure. You linger over dessert in a way that you don't linger over the main course. When you sit down to the main course, hunger pangs are gnawing at our insides and you attack the food with the ferocity and intensity of a starved wolf. You "wolf" your food down. That's what we say. It's right there in Webster's Dictionary. I looked it up to make sure. You wolf your food down.

Then it's time for dessert. You, along with everybody else around the table, relax a bit. You pat your stomach contentedly, push the chair back a little. The coffee's poured, and out comes the dessert. It's a work of art, as in "liberal arts," a feast for the eyes as well as a feast for the palate—colorful, like a painter's palette. You don't want to spoil this work of art all at once. By now your hunger pangs have left anyway. So you eat at a slower pace, leisurely.

That's the way it is with an education in the liberal arts. What are they? They're not just a broad, general education, taking a lot of different subjects. To study the liberal arts is to study those subjects you're free to study because you can take the time to study them—in the case of most of you, four years. You can take the time to study these subjects whether or not studying them is an efficient way of using your time to help you get a job, make more money, or reach an occupational goal. You study them just because they're interesting, just because studying them makes *you* more interesting, just because it makes you less a tool in the workshop, less a cog in the machine, and a more human being, a more *humane* being.

Originally, you see, the liberal arts were called "liberal" because they weren't for slaves. They were the studies that nonslaves, free people, could pursue because they were free of the work that slaves had to do from dawn to dusk. The liberal arts are still for free people, for people with the liberty of leisure to study art and literature, math and science, philosophy and history. The very word "scholarly" means "leisurely." That's the basic meaning of the word. A scholar is a person with leisure.

We're a community of scholars, senior scholars and junior scholars. (I hope you recognize yourselves in that last phrase.) Let us count our blessing of leisure. There was a time when most of us wouldn't have had the liberty of leisure to come to a place like this. One of my grandfathers had to start working the tin mines in Cornwall, England, at a young age and continue mining here in the West when he came to this country. He wasn't a slave in the strict sense. But he wasn't free to pursue a college education, either.

My other grandfather had to drop out of school after fourth grade to help his widowed mother support younger children in the family. Eventually he got married, had four children of his own, moved west, and earned a BA degree through a correspondence course while homesteading a farm in what had been a sagebrush wilderness. I got my first lessons in Greek from a classical Greek grammar book I discovered in that old farmer's bookshelves. He got an education without leisure. But here we sit in one of the most beautiful spots on God's earth—Santa Barbara, California—tasting the dessert of leisure. It's only in the last fifty years or so that a college education has become more or less the norm. Our freedom has expanded to include it.

So don't think of your education here as work. Sure, you'll study. You'll probably study a lot harder than you've ever studied before. You'd better! But don't look on your studying as work, as though you were a slave. This is what you're free to do, what you're at liberty to do. These are the *liberal* arts. You have leisure for them, just as you take your dessert at leisure. We don't give you homework at Westmont. We give you assignments, plenty of them, but no work. We just give you interesting things to do with your leisure time. That's all.

Dessert time isn't only a time of leisure, though. It's also a time of conversation. Just because you take more time eating dessert, you have more time to carry on a conversation. Some conversation goes on during the main part of a dinner, of course. But the sheer quantity of food you consume during that part, and the rate of consumption—they keep you from talking a lot. There's not very much to a dessert, though. So what do you do? You stretch it out. Between bites you talk and talk and talk. And by the time dessert's all gone, you've gotten so much in the mood for talking that you stay at the table, maybe for the whole rest of the evening. The conversation rolls on and on. And that's just what a good college education is: a conversation.

Somebody has called it "The Great Conversation." You converse with Socrates, Plato, and Aristotle. You converse with Jesus and Paul and Augustine, with Shakespeare and Goethe and Faulkner and T. S. Eliot,

Woolf, Sayers, Marx, Freud, Max Weber. When you read their works, they say something to you. When you respond—and their's no true reading without responding—you say something back to them. The silence that's supposed to characterize a library isn't the silence of speechlessness. It's the silence of respect for dozens of conversations that are going on in the library *sub voce*, under the voice. You don't want to disturb these conversations. You don't want to interrupt them.

When you look at a painting by Rembrandt, at a sculpture by Henry Moore, at a building by Frank Lloyd Wright—and when you respond, as respond you must if you truly see what you're looking at—the great conversation keeps going back and forth. The very word "college" comes from two Indo-European roots. One of them has a double meaning: "to reason and talk." The other one means "together." To reason and talk together: that's what a college is, a place for people to reason and talk together.

So talk with people in the past. Talk with your teachers here. Talk with each other as students, not just about surfing and dating and clothes and cars and box scores. Enlarge yourself. Talk with each other about great ideas, important issues, questions of what's good, what's true, what's beautiful (as the ancient Greeks said) or (to use the apostle Paul's words, drawing on the Greeks) what's true, honorable, just, pure, pleasing, commendable, excellent, and praiseworthy (Philippians 4:8).

Don't stay at the shallow end of the pool in your conversation. Go down where the deep water is. Dive in. Join the party. Be a party to this conversation that spans the centuries and circles the globe. Break out of your tiny little world. Become a citizen of the world at large.

Which brings me to my last point. Dessert time isn't only a time of leisure and conversation. As you'd expect from these first two descriptions, it's also a time of enjoyment. You've endured the discipline of eating potatoes and asparagus and turnips in K–12. Now it's time for Santa Barbara Marble Cheesecake, Chocolate Thunder, Lemonberry Jazz, and—just to make it Christian—Angel Food Cake with Strawberries and Whipped Cream. Even the best-satisfied appetites can't resist these delectables. They're delicious! I'm tempted to take time out for seconds right now. These dishes are what you eat the rest of your dinner for.

Desserts are sheer pleasure. And you should regard your Christian college education the same way, as something to enjoy: not only the social life, not only the friends you'll make, not only your extracurricular activities, but also and especially your studies. I say *especially* your studies, because they're what a college specializes in. You can get the other things elsewhere.

Studies a pleasure? you ask. Yes! They hold pleasures and enjoyments that you may never have dreamed exist: the pleasures and enjoyments of developing an appreciation for the differences as well as similarities between human cultures; of learning what it is that makes a mathematical solution, not just correct, but elegant; wherein lies the charm of an Elizabethan sonnet; architectural marvels in the beguiling simplicity of the Parthenon; the psychology of crowd behavior; the delicate and never-ending tension between form and freedom in a work of art, in politics, in morality, in the making of a seemingly impossible shot by Michael Jordan.

Maybe you're laughing on the inside. Maybe you think

I'm weird to talk about taking pleasure in the tensionbetween form and freedom, whatever that means. No matter. I'll have the last laugh, and it won't be a laugh of derision. It'll be a laugh of welcome to the party.

Just don't waste your leisure. Don't sell yourself short, and don't sell short the rest of the human race and the world we all live in. Your enjoyment of life in this world of God's creation will be enhanced immeasurably by delving into the tension between form and freedom, mathematical elegance, and all the other arts, by thinking and talking together about them. You'll discover pleasures sweeter than the frosting on a piece of cake. But only if you approach your college education that way. Only if you treat it as holding the promise of pleasure. Only if you anticipate enjoyment. If you go about it the way you go about eating vegetables, only out of a sense of duty, for you the "dessert" of a college education will lose an "s" and turn into a "desert." Please forgive the spelling lesson while I have another slice of Chocolate Thunder.

Learning for Spiritual Formation

~ Delivered at a convocation ~

Hello and good morning. You may wonder why banners aren't hanging from the rafters, the way they usually do, and why potted plants aren't decorating the platform. Where's the pulpit? And why aren't we starting with a period of silence, some music, and a prayer? We'll pray at the end; but I want to make our time together as little like a chapel service as possible and as much like a class as possible, and I want to make my talk as little like a sermon as possible and as much like a lecture as possible. Before you groan, let me tell you my reason. It grows out of the topic for this morning, "Learning for Spiritual Formation." Learning—that's what you do in class. Chapel—you might learn some things in chapel too. But generally the things you learn in chapel don't represent the kind of learning I have in view, academic learning; and chapel usually aims in other directions anyway: the praise and adoration of God, for example, and exhortation to Christian life and witness. Not academic learning, not in chapel.

Some verses in 1 Corinthians, chapters 14 and 13, provide my text for this lecture. (To suit academic learning I'll call it a lecture.) Here's the text:

> Therefore the person speaking in a tongue is to pray for the gift of interpretation. For if I pray in a tongue, my spirit is praying but my mind is unproductive. What to do, then? I'll pray with the spirit, but I'll also pray with the mind. I'll sing with the spirit, but I'll also sing with the mind. . . . I thank God I speak in tongues more than all of you do; but in church I'd rather speak five words with my mind, to instruct other people, than speak ten thousand words in a tongue. When completeness comes [that is, when maturity comes], what's par-

tial [that is, what's immature] will be discarded.
When I was a child, I talked like a child. I thought
like a child. I reasoned like a child. But now that
I've become an adult, I've discarded childish
things.

I want to do four things in the next few minutes: First, I
want to describe the tug-o'-war that takes place between
learning and spiritual formation. Second, I want to con-
vince you that although the Bible recognizes that tug-o'-
war, the Bible also unites learning and spiritual formation
in a healthy marriage. (Many marriages thrive on a certain
amount of tension, you know.) Third, I want to cite some
personal examples of learning that has contributed to
spiritual formation. Fourth and last, I want to suggest a
couple of ways you can make learning contribute to your
own spiritual formation.

Now let's get straight what "spiritual formation" means or,
more simply, what the word "spiritual" means. It's a word
much in vogue nowadays, a buzz-word. Recently I was
being interviewed on a talk show at KTMS, a local radio
station. The interviewer was a Native American, and a
very nice man. He described himself to me as "spiritual."
What does a man like that mean when he says "spiritual"?
What do more or less secular people mean when they say,
"Oh, Sharon—she's a very spiritual person. So is Fred.
He's spiritual too"? What do they mean by "spiritual"?

They probably mean something like this: "Sharon and Fred
aren't swallowed up by materialism and commercialism.
They pay attention to the other side of life: the inner world
of the human spirit. Not the world of cold, dry reason, but
the world of wonder and beauty and mystery, maybe even
of meditation and a dash of religion (but nothing dogmatic

or doctrinal). Some depth psychology. Perhaps yoga and deep breathing exercises. Certainly a world of friendship and romance, of poetry more than prose, of feelings more than facts."

Now if we baptize that popular meaning of "spiritual" into our Christian vocabulary, we have a problem. "Houston, we have a problem." It's this: since spirituality has to do mainly with feelings, learning can't have very much to do with it. In fact, learning may damage spirituality. There's nothing like studying a college textbook—learning biology from Curtis's *Biology*, or history from Duicker's and Spielvogel's *World History: Comprehensive*, or New Testament background from Barrett's *New Testament Background*—there's nothing like studying a college textbook to dull your feelings and dampen your emotions. So if spirituality has to do mainly with feelings, stay away from the books.

I recently heard a friend of mine say that even though his parents didn't have a higher education, they encouraged him to go to college. Not my parents! Oh, no. They told me, "Don't go to college, not even a Christian one. All that learning will take away your zeal for God. You'll become lukewarm. Your private devotions will suffer. You won't proclaim the gospel to other people as much as you used to." My parents had gone to Biola, you see, before Biola became a college, and a long time before it claimed the title of university. My parents didn't even call it "Biola." They called it "BI," for "Bible Institute." Why would you go to a college and waste your time studying biology and history and literature when you could be studying the Bible, God's Word? And then in my church, time after time after time I heard those tired old jokes in which "PhD" was said to stand for "Post-Hole Digger," and "seminary" was deliberately mispronounced "cemetery." Maybe you've heard those jokes too.

Even learning the Bible is bad for you if it gets academic. Just a couple of weeks ago I heard a preacher as much as say so, and in the process he even mentioned Westmont College by name. You mustn't think that this fear of too much learning, this fear of more and more knowledge— you mustn't think it's limited to fundamentalist Christians like my parents. Not at all. You find it even in the Bible, as well as outside the Bible. It's the fear of forbidden knowledge, knowledge that does you harm. After all, what was the tree called whose fruit Adam and Eve ate when they committed the original sin? "The tree of the knowledge of good and evil." "In the day you eat thereof you shall surely die." And doesn't the New Testament say that God has chosen the foolish things of the world to confound the wise?

Pandora was the original human female in Greek mythology. When she got married, her dowry consisted of a box full of unknown contents. Curiosity got the best of her. She and her husband opened the box, and out flew all the evils and illnesses and misfortunes that afflict the world today. "Curiosity killed the cat." "What you don't know won't hurt you." That's what they say.

"I would I might forget that I am I," wrote the philosopher George Santayana, "and break the heavy chain that holds me fast. . . . Happy the dumb beast, hungering for food, but calling not his suffering his own. . . . Wretched the mortal, pondering his mood, and doomed to know his aching heart alone." Ignorance is bliss. Learning brings sorrow. The story of Frankenstein is a story of forbidden knowledge, the dangers of learning, its tragedy.

In *First Enoch*, a book quoted at length in the New Testament (see Jude 14–15), the evils that led to Noah's Flood are blamed on what nowadays we call the teaching of the liberal arts to human beings. It was the fallen angels who taught them the liberal arts. Fallen angels—so much for Westmont's faculty. At least we had a heavenly past before we fell into teaching you the liberal arts. The technological skills of those who built the Tower of Babel caused the Lord to come down and confuse their language because, as he himself said, "Soon they'll be able to do anything they want." Knowledge is power, and the Lord is a jealous God.

The early Faust exchanged his soul for twenty-four years of knowledge and power, and he landed in hell. In defiance of the gods, Prometheus stole fire from heaven and gave human beings the gift of fire, a symbol of enlightenment; and in punishment for giving them this gift of forbidden knowledge, Prometheus was chained to Mount Caucasus, where every day a vulture tore out his liver and ate it, and the liver grew back each night only to be devoured again the next day. O the risks of spreading knowledge around! J. Robert Oppenheimer supervised the development of the atomic bomb. At MIT, just two years after the bomb was dropped on Hiroshima and Nagasaki, he said, "[We] physicists have known sin; and this is a knowledge which [we] cannot lose." He meant we'd like to lose it, get rid of it; but we can't.

The cloning of Dolly the sheep in Scotland raises the same issue. And just last week we heard a news report that two calves have been cloned in Texas. Is our human quest for learning too dangerous? Dr. Sheer's announcing that he intends to clone a human being exacerbates the question. Whether he does or not is another question, of course. But is our lust for knowledge, including our Christian lust for knowledge, luring us to our own destruction, the way the Sirens, those mythical sea nymphs living on an island off the coast of Italy, lured sailors to destruction with the sweetness of their singing? Are we committing spiritual suicide with our academic learning? My parents said so. Perhaps the best teacher ever to teach at Westmont College, certainly one of the best—her name was Grace King; she taught English literature, and alumni who had her say you could never forget her courses—she agreed with my parents even though she had her own PhD and was brilliant in every way.

And whether you think so or not, many of you probably agree, maybe most of you. You come to chapel to get some relief from learning, don't you? You get your fill of learning in classes, more than your fill. You don't want to hear another lecture, like the one I'm giving right now. And if the chapel speaker reads her message instead of speaking off the cuff, if the message doesn't contain a lot of humor and interesting, touching stories, no matter how well-crafted and profound the message is, you talk about being bored and uninspired. Right? I've heard you say so. With my own ears I've heard you.

Doubtless you've noticed I'm reading this lecture. Yes, I am—deliberately. I'm flaunting my manuscript in front of your eyes. See, here it is. Not that my lecture is particularly well-crafted or profound. I'm just daring you to be bored. That's all. More learning in chapel? You don't want that. Right now, at this very moment, you'd rather be singing and clapping, swinging and swaying, lifting up your hands and dancing in the aisles, than listening to me. It would feel more spiritual, wouldn't it? You want more spirituality: less mind, more motion—more emotion, more *physical* motion, and the more the better.

Don't get me wrong. I'm not knocking those activities; and I'm not criticizing good humor and tender stories, either. Not at all. I'm making a completely different point. It's this: you put listening to lectures, hitting the books, and doing lab work in a separate, distinct category from praying and singing and lifting your hands to the Lord. Things that make you feel mellow or joyful make you feel spiritual too. But things that make your mind work harder—they just don't seem spiritual. They're intellectual, and intellectual isn't spiritual. When it comes right down to it, you're like my parents. You make learning and spirituality enemies of each other. Or if not enemies, at least strangers to each other.

Well, maybe I've exaggerated a bit. If I have, please forgive me. But I do have a point, don't I? Isn't that your tendency? It's mine, I confess. Sure, I feel more spiritual when I'm shedding a tear or singing for joy than when I'm doing research for a paper. Who doesn't? But the question is whether crying and singing actually do make me more spiritual than when I'm pursuing research. Knowledge is dangerous—true. But the fact of the matter is that ignorance is equally dangerous, and the Bible and all human cultures recognize this fact as well. "It isn't good that the soul should be without knowledge" (Proverbs 19:2). "O you fools, be of an understanding heart" (Proverbs 8:5). In the first chapter of Proverbs, Lady Wisdom shouts to the crowds in the streets and marketplaces, "Won't you ever stop sneering and laughing at knowledge? . . . when you're struck by some terrible disaster, or when trouble and distress surround you like a whirlwind, I'll laugh and make fun of you. You'll ask for my help, but I won't listen. . . . you wouldn't learn."

But it's not just that ignorance is as dangerous to spirituality as knowledge is. And it's not just that you can learn things without losing your spirituality. It's that spirituality—true, deep spirituality—*requires* knowledge. It requires learning. Why, the very word "disciple" means "learner." It doesn't mean "follower," as you've often heard—mistakenly. It's true that disciples followed their teacher, literally followed him, tagged along behind him. But the word itself, "disciple," means "learner." So Jesus says, "Take my yoke upon you, and learn from me" (Matthew 11:29). "Go make disciples," Jesus says in the Great Commission; "make learners of all the nations, . . . teaching them" (Matthew 28:19). And Paul writes, "In him [Christ] are hidden all the treasures of wisdom and knowledge" (Colossians 2:3). He also writes that you should have your "mind renewed so that you may demonstrate [in your life] the will of God, [that is,] what's good and pleasing and mature" (Romans 12:2).

"What's good and pleasing and mature"—that sounds a lot like the ancient Greek trio of "the good, the true, and the beautiful." And, Paul says, the renewing of your mind is part of your "spiritual service of worship" (Romans 12:1). At least that's what most of our English translations have. But in this passage the word that Paul uses for "spiritual" is *logikên*, from which we get "logical." In other words, the renewing of our minds is a spiritually rational exercise in contrast with the merely physical or emotional, or the irrational. And Peter uses the same expression when he tells us to "desire, as newborn babies, the pure, spiritual milk," that is, "the rational milk" which will make us "grow up" (1 Peter 2:2).

You've often heard that according to Jesus, the most important commandment is to love God with all your heart, soul, strength, and mind (Mark 12:30). What's not often pointed out is that Jesus is quoting Deuteronomy 6:5, but the word "mind" isn't there in Deuteronomy. Jesus adds it to the Old Testament text. And when in Mark's version the commandment is quoted a second time, the word "understanding" creeps in (love God "with all your understanding"), because understanding comes from using your mind. Deuteronomy doesn't have "understanding," either. The New Testament adds that word, just as it adds the word "mind."

It was the early Christian theologian Tertullian who asked the question, "What has Jerusalem to do with Athens? What compatibility is there between the Academy and the Church?" He meant, what does biblical revelation, represented by Jerusalem, have to do with Greek rationality, represented by Athens? In other words, what does the gospel have to do with higher education? Well, Tertullian, just read your New Testament. It deliberately adds the Greek term "mind" to a Jewish text that didn't originally have it. And Paul's command in Philippians 4:8 to make your mind dwell on whatever is true and serious and right and pure and charming and reputable and virtuous and praiseworthy—Paul's command looks like a page torn straight out of a hellenistic handbook of moral philosophy, such as some of you are reading right about now in Barrett's *New Testament Background*.

Even earliest Christianity represented a wedding of the mind with the heart, of rationality with feeling, of reason with emotion. Look at the apostle Paul's discussion of spiritual gifts for spiritual people, the text I read for you earlier. Talk about a passage that deals with spirituality!

But Paul doesn't call the gifts spiritual because they arise out of our own spirits. And Paul doesn't call some people spiritual because they cultivate their own spirits. No, Paul calls the gifts spiritual because they're given by the Holy Spirit; and he calls some people spiritual because they're filled with the Holy Spirit. So spiritual formation doesn't mean just the formation of your human spirit. At least that's not the main meaning, or it shouldn't be. Your human spirit isn't the object of formation so much as it is God's Spirit who *does* the forming.

First and foremost, then, spiritual formation means the Holy Spirit's forming you—all of you, including your mind, not just your spirit, because Paul says that if you have the gift of tongues you should pray for the gift of interpretation, too, lest your spirit pray but your mind be unproductive. "I'll pray with the spirit, but I'll also pray with the mind!" Paul exclaims. "I'll sing with the spirit, but I'll also sing with the mind! . . . I'd rather speak five words with my mind than ten thousand words in a tongue." Then he goes on to say, "Stop being little children in your thinking . . . . Instead, be mature in your thinking." And in discussing love, which expresses itself through spirituality, through exercising your spiritual gifts—in discussing love, Paul says, "When I was a child, I talked like a child. I thought like a child. I reasoned like a child. But now that I've become an adult, I've discarded childish things." That's what we're trying to get ourselves to do here at Westmont! To grow up. To become adults. To stop thinking and talking and acting like children. To exercise our powers of reason like mature human beings. To live up to the meaning of *homo sapiens*. *Sapiens* means "knowing." *Homo sapiens*—a knowing human, a creature who has knowledge, who learns, thinks, uses his or her mind.

Forget all that fluff you've heard about simple, childlike faith. When Jesus said to become like little children, he wasn't referring to the way children believe without thinking, without asking questions. You'll find out soon enough that children do ask questions, lots of them. Jesus was referring to the humble position of children in his culture, quite unlike their exalted position in the youth-dominated culture where we live. Take a lowly position, like that of a child, he was saying. But when it comes to believing and thinking and feeling, when it comes to your mind and emotions, grow up. Only then will you love effectively and meaningfully. Otherwise your love becomes sappy and soupy and transient. It won't have depth or permanence. And your emotions will suffer, too, because unless your spirituality matures through learning, you'll never enjoy the depth of feeling that a person of mental substance enjoys.

A beautiful piece of music touches the heartstrings of a person who knows music much more deeply than it does a musical ignoramus. A fine object of art speaks to a person who knows art much more eloquently than to an illiterate in art. The reason is that, in the end, you really can't separate the mind and the emotions. You really can't separate reason and feeling. They go together. Stay childish in one and you'll stay childish in the other. Grow up in one and you'll grow up in the other. If I don't like a classic piece of music, whether it's Mozart or jazz (I almost said, whether it's Bach or rock—then I decided I'd better stick with music; but for those of you who're convinced that rock really is music, I'm only making myself an illustration of the point)—if I don't like a classic piece of music, if it bores me, leaves me cold, the reason isn't that there's something wrong with the music. There's something wrong with me. I'm ignorant. I'm deficient. I'm childish. The same goes for a great piece of art or literature, an elegant solution in mathematics, an argument in philosophy, an experiment in chemistry. I'm uninterested, not because it's uninteresting, but because I haven't learned enough to be interested in something that's inherently very interesting, even exciting.

Why do you think we still read C. S. Lewis with profit and enjoyment? Take his science fiction, his children's fairy stories, the Narnia Series, or his book, *The Four Loves*? What gave these books their staying power, so that people read them now even more than when Lewis was alive? I'll tell you the answer: he incorporated his great learning into his spirituality. It deepened his spirituality. You see, before he wrote *The Four Loves*, Lewis wrote a scholarly book, *Allegory of Love: A Study in Medieval Tradition*. And as he was writing *The Screwtape Letters*, *Mere Christianity*, the Narnia Series, and other Christian books, he was writing *Preface to Paradise Lost* and *English Literature in the Sixteenth Century*. The learning that produced these scholarly, technical books made his popular Christian books weighty enough to stand the test of time.

Or take Blaise Pascal. He was a mathematician and physicist as well as a philosopher and master of French prose. He laid the foundation for the modern theory of probabilities. His law of pressure led him to invent the syringe and the hydraulic press. And he was a Christian. Why do people still read his *Pensées* (French for *Thoughts*) even though he died over three hundred years ago at the age of thirty-nine? You'll find his book down at Border's or Chaucer's or any other secular bookstore worth its salt, not just in Christian bookstores. In fact, you'll stand a better chance in secular bookstores than in Christian ones, given the froth and foam that, sad to say, ooze off the shelves of many Christian bookstores nowadays. What draws people to Pascal's *Thoughts*? It's the profundity of his thoughts. Even when his Christian thoughts weren't related directly to his math and physics, his great learning in those fields gave him a habit of thinking deeply about the Christian faith too; so we still read him, and feel ourselves spiritually formed when we do.

Here's someone we don't read anymore, but do we ever feel the effects of his ministry! I'm referring to John Wesley. He was a travelling evangelist, the founder of the Methodist denomination. In his prime he averaged 15–20 miles a day on horseback, preached 3–5 times every day of the week, and spent hours in prayer. In other words, he was what you'd call SPIRITUAL, in capital letters. Yet in his *Journal*, which runs to several big volumes, he tells us, "History, philosophy, and poetry I read on horseback, having other employments at other times." And not just light reading, either. Paging through his *Journal* at random, I found references to *Belisarius's Life of* [Pope] *Sixtus V* and Joseph Priestly's *Treatise on Electricity*. Nor did Wesley confine himself to reading on horseback. He also composed his own poetry, but not in English so much as in Greek hexameter. I also ran across quotations, apparently from memory, of Homer and Plato and Lucian, all in the original Greek, and of Virgil and Ovid, in the original Latin. He talks about reading the early church fathers, like Ephraem the Syrian. He even read the writings of the early church fathers to his converts in their private living rooms. Can you imagine a present-day evangelist (or pastor, for that matter) making housecalls to read passages out of Justin Martyr, Irenaeus, Athanasius, and other fathers to ordinary church members? Wesley did. For himself he regularly read the Old Testament in Hebrew and the New Testament in Greek. He studied German and French and Spanish. He not only studied them. He wrote a German grammar. He wrote a French grammar. He wrote a French dictionary. He wrote a Hebrew grammar. He wrote an English dictionary. He translated German hymns into English. He wrote several books of history (a history of England and a history of Rome, for example), a book on logic, another book on medicine. He edited the works of other authors, and a magazine. All in all, he authored, translated, and edited over two hundred works. The Wesleyan Revival that came out of the spiritual formation of this learned man, who wedded his mind to his heart— that revival of over two hundred years ago is a very large part of the reason Westmont College exists today as an evangelical Christian institution.

And if you want examples of Christian women who've wedded their minds to their hearts, all you have to do is look around you at our faculty. We have some remarkable examples, and you know who they are. Look up to them. Treasure them. Emulate them. And in saying so, I'm addressing you males as much as females.

You're getting the idea of learning for spiritual formation, I hope. Not just learning the Bible and theology for spiritual formation, but learning *everything* you learn so that the Holy Spirit may form you into a substantial person who can make a profound impact for the kingdom of God. I don't suppose any of us will turn out to be a Wesley, Pascal, or Lewis, though we never can tell. Some of you may surprise us! I'm not, emphatically not, implying it takes an intellectual giant to be a spiritual giant. Learning the liberal arts isn't the only kind of learning the Holy Spirit can use for spiritual formation, and the history of the church is full of examples very different from the ones I've mentioned. But we're a college; and if God has called you here, he's called you here to learn the liberal arts so that the Holy Spirit may use them to form you, transform you by renewing your mind, and conform you to the image of Christ. So relate your learning to that kind of formation.

If you're studying Kinesiology, think of yourself as a spiritual athlete. The apostle Paul regularly uses athletic metaphors for Christian living; and stretching through the centuries there's a long, rich tradition of Christians as spiritual athletes. The tradition began with Jesus himself, agonizing in the Garden of Gethsemane. Agony is an old Greek word for an athletic contest. Jesus was wrestling in prayer. Prayer takes effort. Conversational prayer is almost an oxymoron. To pray is to wrestle, as Jacob did, even earlier than Jesus, wrestling with the angel of the Lord and gaining a blessing. Paul talked about his own wrestling in prayer, and also about running the Christian race. Kinesiology should translate into spiritual training, spiritual discipline, spiritual practice, using the means of grace the way you use athletic equipment in the Fitness Center. If it doesn't, you're not letting your learning of Kinesiology contribute to your spiritual formation.

Or take the learning of rhetoric in Communication Studies. Rhetoric has to do with the use of words or, as one of our professors says, "loving appropriately through speech." The great North African bishop Saint Augustine had been a teacher of rhetoric. Listen to the way he brings his knowledge of rhetoric into a Christmas sermon on the divine Word, now incarnate in Jesus Christ:

> It isn't at all strange that . . . human speech [is] inadequate when we undertake to praise . . . the Word of God . . . as he exists in the bosom of the Father. . . . For how would our tongue be able to

> pay suitable tribute to him? . . . It isn't strange . . .
> for us to fail to find words with which to speak of
> the Word by whom the word was spoken that gave
> existence to us. . . . For our mind brings words into
> existence after they've been thought over and
> formed, but our mind itself is formed by the Word.

Augustine doesn't use rhetoric merely to say something
appropriately or eloquently. No, he makes rhetoric the very
subject matter of what he has to say about Jesus, God's
Word, God's communication to us. Jesus is God's rhetoric,
making all our rhetoric possible and then overwhelming it
when it comes to our speaking of him. So what Augustine
has to say is a lot more satisfying than superficial
Christmas sermons about how hard it must have been for
pregnant Mary to ride a donkey to Bethlehem (of course,
we don't know she did ride a donkey!), or how hard it was
for her to endure hometown gossip about her questionable
pregnancy.

If you want to talk about Mary at Christmastime, consider
these words, which Ephraim the Syrian put in her mouth:

> Your home, my Son, is higher than all, yet it was
> your wish to make me your home. Heaven is too
> small to contain your splendor; yet I, poorest of
> creatures, am carrying you. Let Ezekiel come and
> see you on my knees. Let him kneel down and
> worship you, and acknowledge it was you he saw
> there lifted up by the cherubim above the chariot
> [remember Ezekiel's vision in which he saw God's
> chariot with wheels within wheels?] and let
> [Ezekiel] call me blessed who carry you now. The
> very chariot stops, amazed that I carry its Master. . . .
> my bosom is your home! Your radiance rests on my
> knees, the throne of your majesty is held in my

> arms. Instead of the chariot wheels, my fingers clasp you. . . . Come, all you who have discernment . . . you prophets who beheld hidden things in your true visions; you farmers who sowed seed and slept in hope, rise up and rejoice at the harvest. Look, in my arms I clasp the wheat-sheaf of life that provides bread for the hungry, that feeds the needy! Rejoice with me, for I carry the sheaf full of joys!

Now that's spirituality infused with rhetoric! And if you don't learn to infuse rhetoric into your spirituality, you're failing the very purpose of taking Communication Studies at a Christian liberal arts college.

In my original draft I included another suggestion for Econ and Business majors. Then I scrapped it, because it didn't seem to illustrate what I'm getting at. Now I'm going to reintroduce it, but as a counter-example, an example of what I *don't* mean. Here it is: if you're studying Econ and Business, don't study them to better yourself. As a Christian, study Econ and Business to serve the public better. One of my jobs when earning my way through college and seminary was working in Hinshaw's department store at the Quad in Whittier. The store isn't there any more, but Hinshaw himself was a very successful businessman. Earlier in his life he'd managed a whole chain of department stores throughout the Northwest; and at one time, when working for Montgomery Ward in New York City, he'd been among the highest-paid CEOs in the USA. Yet everywhere I went in his store at the Quad, I'd see little signs posted on the desks of the clerks. The wording differed from sign to sign, but the gist was always the same: Remember, it's more important to serve the needs of our customers than to increase our profits.

Hinshaw had grown up an evangelical Quaker and was infusing Christian spirituality, the spirituality of serving others, into his business practice. But that's not my point this morning. It's not to work Christianity into your business. It's not to work spirituality into your learning. You should, of course. You should make your learning an act of worship by putting a Christian perspective on the literature you study, on the art, on the psychology, on the sociology, the political science—on whatever you study. Sometimes it'll be easy to do, sometimes hard to do. How do you put a Christian perspective on math? I don't know. Maybe our math teachers can tell us. But this morning isn't about putting spirituality into learning, about infusing our learning with spirituality. It's the other way around. It's about putting learning into spirituality, about infusing spirituality with learning, so that our spirituality will have density and depth and weight, so that our spirituality is thoughtful and wise and knowledgeable as well as warm and glowing and tender. Learning for spiritual formation means working everything you learn, in all your courses, working it into your Christian life and witness instead of keeping it separate from your spirituality. Instead of walling off your spirituality and keeping it supposedly safe from your learning, pray the Holy Spirit to make your learning nourish your spirituality, your Christian life, your Christian witness.

I've talked long enough. You can figure out other examples of learning the liberal arts for spiritual formation. So let me close with a scriptural passage, plus a Greek myth. In Colossians 3:12–14 the Apostle Paul writes, "Therefore as God's chosen ones, holy and beloved, clothe yourselves with emotions of pity, with generosity, humility, meekness, patience, putting up with each other and showing grace to each other, just as also the

Lord showed grace to you. . . . and over all these traits put love, which is the bond of maturity." In other words, love is the belt that binds together all these other articles of clothing, the virtues of Christian character, and makes them an integrated whole.

Now the Greek myth. It's one I've already referred to—about the Sirens, those sea nymphs who wooed sailors to destruction with the sweetness of their singing. Odysseus was sailing home with his men after the Trojan War. They approached the rocky shores of the Sirens' island. Someone warned Odysseus what was liable to happen, what *had* happened to many other sailors, whose bleached bones lay scattered about the island. So Odysseus stuck wax in the ears of his men. That way they wouldn't hear the singing of the Sirens. Then he had his men bind him so tightly to the ship's mast that even though he could hear the sweet singing of the Sirens, he couldn't break loose to steer the ship toward the island. As they sailed past, then, Odysseus heard the singing and savoured its beauty, but he didn't succumb to its fatal attraction. He was bound by the cords of love for Penelope, his faithful wife who'd waited for him twenty years back home. In the same way, our liberal arts hold charms that could prove fatally attractive. They could diminish or destroy our spirituality. But we can savor them safely, and—more than that—learn them to the enrichment of our spirituality, if we're bound with the cords of love for our ever faithful God, who's waiting for us to come home. "You shall love the Lord your God with all your heart, with all your soul, with all your strength, and with all your mind." Let us pray, with some help from a slightly revised version of a prayer by Isaac Watts:

> Great God, when you descend within our view
> You charm our reason to pursue,

But leave it tired and fainting in th' unequal chase.
Or if we reach unusual height
Till near your presence brought,
There, floods of glory check our flight,
Cramp the bold pinions of our wit,
And all untune our thought.
Plunged in a sea of light, we roll
Where wisdom, justice, mercy shines;
Infinite rays in crossing lines
Beat thick confusion on our sight,
And o'erwhelm our soul.
Great God, behold our reason lies
Adoring: yet our love would rise
On pinions not her own.
Faith shall direct her humble flight,
Through all the trackless seas of light
To thee, th' Eternal Fair, through Christ made
    known.
Amen.

Shredding the Bible

~ Delivered in retrospect of an art show
and in prospect of a guest lecture ~

With a title like that, we need to pray. So let's start with a prayer out of the past, a prayer to God the Father:

> The prayers I make will then be sweet indeed,
> If thou the Spirit give by which I pray.
> My unassisted heart is barren clay,
> Which of its native self can nothing feed.
> Of good and godly works thou art the seed
> Which enlivens where thou say'st it may.
> Unless thou show us then thine own true way,
> No one can find it! Father, Thou must lead!
> Please, then, breathe those thoughts into my mind
> By which such virtue may in me be bred
> That in thy holy footsteps I may tread.
> The fetters of my tongue do thou unbind,
> That I may have the power to sing of thee
> And sound thy praises everlastingly.

That prayer comes from the all-time great sixteenth-century artist Michelangelo.

Last December 1st our student newspaper, *The Horizon*, carried an article with the headline, "Faith Challenged Though Controversial Art." That was a spelling mistake, of course. The headline should have read, "Faith Challenged *Through* Controversial Art." The article featured a work created by Linda Ekstrom and displayed at our own Reynolds Gallery in the fifth annual Christmas show of art that has become traditional here at Westmont College. This particular work won the award, "Best of Show."

Along with the article about the work of art, *The Horizon* ran a photograph of the work. Here it is in another photograph. You can see the Best of Show ribbon over on the right.

The art object itself consists of a Bible whose pages have been shredded so as to portray an angel, and *The Horizon* reported that Professor Tony Askew had described this piece as "the most visually angelic" in the whole show. Now I wouldn't dare contradict that judgment of my friend and colleague, partly because he has an artist's eye and I don't, and partly because I've never seen an angel, at least not knowingly, except for my wife and daughters and grandchildren, of course; and this piece of art doesn't at all look like them.

But according to *The Horizon*, the visual effect, whatever it is for you, was achieved by the artist's cutting up the Bible ten pages at a time, line by line, though the resulting strips of paper are still attached at the spine. I suppose you could ask whether exercising some technical artistic mastery, as well as having a genuinely creative idea, is necessary for a serious work of art and, if so, whether the ability to cut paper with a pair of scissors meets the standard of technical artistic mastery. I don't know the answer to that question. I really don't, and I'm not equipped to discuss it. But I do know that some people would say, maybe *have* said, "This work of art is a sacrilege, a desecration of the Holy Bible! What's it doing hanging in our art gallery? Aren't we supposed to be Christian? Why, in my home we didn't even stack another book on top of the Bible, much less shred the Bible with a pair of scissors. Blasphemy!"

This is a college, though. People at a college aren't supposed to give knee-jerk reactions. If this shredded Bible is a serious work of art—and being judged "Best of Show" indicates some expert opinion that it is—we need to treat it seriously, not just dismiss it with a simple-minded, disgusted "Harrumph!"

The artist says, "My Protestant friends really haven't had much trouble [with this piece of art]." What an irony! The first Protestants proclaimed, "*Sola Scriptura*! The Scriptures alone have the authority to govern our beliefs and actions." Yet here you have Protestants who've lost their protest: it doesn't bother them very much that their Bible is being shredded like some embarrassing memo in the White House.

But the artist says that her Jewish friends—ah, they do have trouble with her shredding the Bible (I suppose she means that part of it we Christians call the Old Testament) because for Jews, as she says, the Word of God "takes on a presence and power you do not destroy." Presumably, even secular Jews would wince at shredding the Bible, though for them it's only a cultural artifact: it's *their* cultural artifact; after all, and it represents a belief that's important in their history despite the fact they themselves don't believe anymore that the Bible is God's Word.

Of course, the artist doesn't see herself as destroying the Bible. Neither did the judge of the show, Sherry Frumkin. She described the making of this art object as an act of faith: the artist trusts the Bible so much that she's "willing to take the leap of imagination," confident that shredding the Bible won't "bring it down." It's people weak in faith who think "tearing the pages of a book can bring it down." That's the judge's verdict. The artist herself says, "I'm presenting the Bible in a new way." And again the judge: "It is possible to see that this book [the Bible] has not been sullied [or defiled], but rather transformed . . . its spirit unbroken, undiminished." I hope there's no allusion to Omar Khayyam's "Rubaiyat": "My head is bloodied but unbowed." I don't think so. In any case, the spirit of the Bible seems to replace the meaning of the Bible. (I mean "meaning" in the broad sense that includes law and wisdom and liturgy and devotion and what the Bible itself calls "the beauty of holiness" as well as supposedly abstract theology.) The meaning of the Bible may be broken and diminished by this work of art, but its spirit isn't. So said the judge of the art show.

And what is the spirit of the Bible? The artist provides an answer of her own. Among other things she says, "I'm very interested in the Bible as an inspirational book." You'll notice that the very word "spirit" lies at the center of the word "inspirational." Now who could argue with that statement? On second thought, I can think of people who *would* argue with it. They don't take much inspiration from the genealogies in Genesis and Chronicles, Matthew and Luke, from the blueprint of the tabernacle in Exodus, the laws of sacrifice and purity in Leviticus, the slaughter of the Canaanites in Joshua, the lake of fire in Revelation. Fear? Yes. Horror? Yes. Sheer boredom? Yes. But inspiration? No. As my five-year old son said when we were reading the laws of sacrifice in the early chapters of Leviticus for family devotions, "Of what interest is all this to me?" Not much, so for his sake we skipped to Joshua, where at least you have some blood and thunder. Still, most people find large parts of the Bible inspirational. But Christians have always believed the Bible to be inspired as well as inspiring, inspired by God's Spirit, not just inspiring to human beings. So this object of art really does present the Bible in a new way, as inspiring without being inspired.

Am I being fair, though? The artist doesn't deny the Bible is inspired. She just affirms that it's inspiring. True, but let me defend my criticism. I haven't told you the title that the artist gave her creation. It's "Sophia/Logos." *Sophia* is the Greek word for "wisdom." *Logos* is the Greek word for "word," as in the famous statements at the start of John's Gospel: "In the beginning was the Word [*Logos*], and the Word was with God, and the Word was God . . . . the Word became flesh and dwelt among us." And this Word, whom John calls "a one-and-only [who was] God, the one existing in the bosom of [God] the Father—that one has expressed him [or as we might translate it, 'demystified him']."

How then does *Sophia*, "Wisdom," get into the picture alongside *Logos*, "Word"? Well, most scholars think nowadays that John personified *Logos*, the Word as Jesus Christ, on the basis of Jewish literature, including the Old Testament, that had already personified wisdom—Lady Wisdom, because *Sophia* is a feminine noun, as in Sophia Loren. But since Jesus was a man, not a woman, John switched over to *Logos*, which is masculine, and said the same things about Jesus the *Logos*, the Word, that were already being said about Lady Wisdom, *Sophia*. So our artist has displayed considerable theological sophistication, perhaps even a bit of feminist theology, by titling her work "Sophia/Logos."

There's irony in the title, though. *Logos* means not only "word." It also means "reason" or "rationality." And *sophia* literature, wisdom literature, is the closest you come to reason and rationality in the Old Testament and apocrypha. Yet the artist says that although "we access [the Bible] intellectually, through rational capacities," her work of art presents the Bible in "a nonrational way." So the title "Sophia/Logos" doesn't really fit its object. The title shouts, "Wisdom, Word, Reason, *Rational* Discourse." The art object shouts back, "*Non*rationality." And you can see how it does. Just look at it. You can't read a Bible shredded up like this one. You can't make sense of it any more than you could make sense of the Bible if it were printed on the strands of a dust mop. In this state, the Bible doesn't make theological sense. It doesn't make emotional sense. It doesn't make worshipful sense. It doesn't make any sense.

There's even deeper irony. Words get much of their meaning from their contexts. Take the word "spirit," for example. I mentioned it earlier. Does it mean God's Spirit, the human spirit, an angelic spirit, a demonic spirit, an alcoholic beverage, a mood, enthusiasm (as in "school spirit"), an underlying principle (as in "the spirit of the law" as opposed to its letter)? Only the context will tell you. But shredding the Bible destroys most of the context of its words and therefore destroys most of their meaning. So *Logos* loses not only its meaning "reason" or "rationality." It also loses its meaning "word." All we have here is words, words, words but no overarching word that conveys a message.

But we still haven't done with irony. This art object won the best of show award in a Christmas exhibition called "Un Ange Passe." That's French for "An angel is passing by." We associate angels especially with Christmas because of the annunciations by Gabriel and the angel of the Lord, and because of the angelic choir singing outside Bethlehem. Now the word "angel" means "messenger, the bearer of a message." Yet this angel, the angel of this art work, is a contradiction in terms. It bears no message. The message as well as the messenger has been shredded to pieces. The only thing binding those pieces together is a wordless spine.

It was only natural, then, for the artist to describe her process of shredding the Bible "as very much like a ritual." Here, ritual *substitutes* for the meaning of God's Word instead of *dramatizing* its meaning and thereby *enhancing* that meaning. So *The Horizon* correctly observed, "A maroon marker drops through the mass of disheveled paper strips and hangs gracefully against the stark white block which supports the piece." The marker has no meaningful function any more. It's supposed to mark the place where you stopped reading so you can take it up again in a meaningful progression. But you can't read this Bible. So the marker functions only to provide some color (maroon) and even then not in the Bible, only outside the Bible, because although the Bible is open, it's uselessly open. The mass of disheveled paper strips hides the colored marker till it drops below the Bible against the table top.

But there's more than one way to shred the Bible. So I ask the question, Are we shredding the Bible at Westmont College? Are we shredding the Bible in biology courses, in psychology courses, in English courses? Most of all, are we shredding the Bible in religious studies courses? Am I shredding the Bible when teaching Life and Literature of the New Testament, for example?

I have to ask myself that question when a student comes into my office and says: I used to love reading my Bible. But I don't any more. I don't even read it any more. It's a problem to me. All I can think of is that the ancient manuscripts don't always agree on the exact wording, and the English translations aren't always right, and they disagree with each other anyway, and Matthew leaves out of Jesus' genealogy four generations that we know of from the Old Testament and probably a number more between the testaments, and Mark quotes the Aramaic Targum and the Greek Septuagint translations of the Old Testament even where they disagree with the original Hebrew, and Matthew puts the cleansing of the temple on Palm Sunday but Mark puts it the next day, Monday of Passion Week, and John three and a half years earlier, and Luke puts the Sermon on the Mount at the base of a mountain, and the Gospel of John has Jesus proclaiming his own identity all over the place while the other Gospels have him keeping his messiahship secret, and Paul quotes some passages out of Hosea as though they speak about Gentiles when they really have to do with Israel, and scholars disagree whether he wrote all the letters that begin with his name and that I've always assumed he wrote, and Jude quotes a book falsely written under the name of Enoch. I'm so confused. You've shredded the Bible for me. You've spoiled it. You've killed it. How do you expect me to get anything out of it? I can't even read it any more without thinking of questions, questions, questions, problems, problems, problems.

I know exactly how you feel. One day in Manchester, England, I was studying the way Matthew uses the Old Testament. It looked to me as though he was abusing it more than using it, what with all his changing of the text and applying it to all sorts of things that the Old Testament writers obviously never had in mind. So I said out loud, even though I was alone at the time—I said, "God, it's not looking good for you and your book." But here I am teaching it at Westmont College. What happened?

Well, facts are facts; so I couldn't change them. Matthew really does take big liberties with the Old Testament. It really is true that Jude quotes *1 Enoch* (so-called), that the authorship of 2 Peter is debated, and so on. I can't change those facts. You can't. Nobody can. We could play ostrich and hide our heads in the sand, of course; but our rumps would still be exposed, and facts have a way of kicking people in the seat of their pants. So what happened that I ended up here instead of chucking the whole thing, or if not the Christian faith at least the academic study of the Bible that gives us so much anxiety?

The answer didn't lie in changing my view of the Bible as God's Word. It lay in growing up intellectually, coming to distinguish between beliefs that are crucial and beliefs that are negotiable, and, perhaps above all, in learning some hermeneutics. Hermeneutics? you ask. Yes, hermeneutics—not the technology of making things airtight, but the science and art of interpretation, after the Greek god Hermes, messenger and interpreter of the other gods.

Let me go back to our art object and give it a brief reinterpretation, an interpretation much more favorable than the one I gave earlier, though with apologies to the artist this new interpretation will require a change in the title. You'll remember that the artist cut ten pages at a time so as to keep the lines readable. In other words, she had to cut straight to keep from destroying the lines by cutting through them. Now it so happens that the Bible itself talks about cutting the Word of God straight. 2 Timothy 2:15: "Study to show yourself approved to God, a worker who doesn't need to be ashamed, cutting the word of truth straight." The old King James Version of the Bible has "rightly dividing the word of truth," and some people used to think that Paul was telling us to divide up the Bible into different dispensations, or ages, like the dispensation of human innocence in the Garden of Eden, or the age of the Law from Moses to Christ, and the age of grace at the present time.

But the verb really means to cut straight, and it's used as a figure of speech for correct interpretation, so that the NRSV has "rightly explaining the word of truth." I'd like to retitle this art object, "The Straight Cut," then—not "*A* Straight Cut," such as you'd get at a hair salon, a cut without a wash or a perm, but "*The* Straight Cut," which stands for cutting the Word of God straight, understanding it aright, interpreting the Bible correctly.

"Shredding" is the wrong word, you see. It means to tear off a strip irregularly. But our artist hasn't done that. She has cut the pages, and cut them very carefully, in straight lines. Now you can see the Word of God, not just two facing pages at a time, as in a standard Bible, but many, many lines at a time, all still attached to each other to form a single, sacred canon. One angel, "Une Ange," one message. The maroon marker doesn't dichotomize the Bible any more. The divisive marker is overwhelmed with what Isaiah calls "the word of the Lord . . . line upon line, line upon line, here a little, there a little" (Isaiah 28:13).

And the multiplicity of lines shows that the one message has great variety, enough to meet our different needs. It's a message of many stripes, just as this is a Bible of many strips. The object of art should teach us to value variation in the Bible as an enrichment of God's revelation rather than a problem for it. The Bible isn't neat and tidy. It's messy or, to use *The Horizon*'s less vulgar description, "disheveled." But that's OK. This text has texture. Don't try to level it out. It's richer if you don't. Revel in its richness, in its profundity, in its diversity. Prosaic accuracy and poetic license, moralistic advice and racy stories, fact and fiction, and much more—all of them true in their own ways.

The Bible isn't just for logicians. It's for artists and plumbers, too, doctors and lawyers, housewives and carpenters, slum-dwellers, suburbanites, aborigines, readers of *The National Enquirer* as well as readers of *The New York Times*. There's something for everybody. A line for you. A line for me. We may not know just how all the lines fit together, just as we can't see how all the lines fit together in this art object. But somehow behind that tumbled mass of lines the Angel of the Lord, hidden from our view for the moment, is holding the lines together. Now we see in part. Someday we'll see in whole, with no need to cut the lines straight, or to cut them at all, because interpretation will give way to direct encounter.

What I've given you this morning is a Protestant evangelical account of what happens, or should happen, when we discover the Bible as it really is, in black and white (red letter editions are an abomination), in some contrast with the Bible as it exists only in our imaginations. But what would a Catholic Christian say? As those of you who've taken theology know, both Eastern and Western Catholics set church tradition alongside the Bible. Eastern Catholics freeze that tradition, at least the infallible part of it, in the eighth century with the seventh ecumenical council. Western Catholics, Roman Catholics, keep that tradition growing right up through the present. So for Catholics, the Bible doesn't mean simply what it says. It means what the church has said it means and, especially in the case of Roman Catholics, what the church continues to say it means.

Now as providence would have it, this Friday in chapel we're going to have a Roman Catholic speaking to us on this very topic. In fact, what I've done here is supposed to set the stage for his presentation. He's going to talk on the topic, "The Extraordinary Encounter of Roman Catholicism with the Bible in the 20th Century," and his name is Raymond Brown. He'd be on everybody's list of the top ten New Testament scholars in the world today. As an undergraduate, he was Phi Beta Kappa. He earned an M.A. in philosophy from the Catholic University of America in Washington, D.C., a Doctorate of Sacred Theology from St. Mary's Seminary and University in Baltimore, another doctorate, a PhD in Semitic languages, at the Johns Hopkins University, also in Baltimore, and a License in Sacred Scripture from the Pontifical Biblical Commission in Rome, where he also studied at the Gregorian University. He holds 26 honorary doctorates from the likes of the universities of Glasgow and Edinburgh, Scotland, Uppsala, Sweden, and Louvain, Belgium, as well as from numerous American universities. And he's the first person ever to have been elected president of all three of the distinguished societies, the Catholic Biblical Association, the Society of Biblical Literature (the largest society of biblical scholars in the world), and the international Studiorum Novi Testamenti Societas (the Society of New Testament Studies). Tomorrow evening he's lecturing at 7:30 in Porter Hall on the passion and death of Jesus, about which he has recently written a huge two-volume work.

But in Friday's chapel, as I said, he'll speak on "The Extraordinary Encounter of Roman Catholicism with the Bible in the 20th Century." Roman Catholics have run into some of the same questions about the Bible that we Protestant evangelicals have. So it'll be revealing, maybe even rewarding, to hear what Father Brown has to say. Of course, most of us have come to these questions from a different angle. We've been preoccupied with the Bible, not to say fixated on it. Away with tradition! Back to the Bible! Whereas Roman Catholics accept the authority of tradition as well as biblical authority.

So if I were you, I'd be asking myself while Father Brown speaks, Are these questions about the Bible more serious for me, do they cause me more existential despair than they do him, because the Bible doesn't mean quite so much to him as to me? He can always fall back on church tradition, but for me the Bible is all or nothing. Or is it rather that like Roman Catholics I too have a tradition? It has made me understand the Bible in certain ways, and now that I know the Bible better I have to change some of those ways of understanding it even while I keep on believing it to be God's Word. Maybe it's not the Bible I'm giving up, but certain parts of my tradition.

Is the Bible correcting my tradition just as it has been correcting Roman Catholic tradition, if it *has* been correcting that tradition? Will Father Brown tell us that the Bible has been correcting Roman Catholic tradition, or only that Roman Catholic tradition about the Bible has been evolving, developing? Correction would seem to undermine the authority of church tradition, wouldn't it? Development might sound a little more benign. And how much change can our traditions tolerate without tearing the Bible to shreds and throwing our faith into a tailspin? Are

Roman Catholics becoming more like liberal Protestants who don't have much faith in the Bible any longer, or more like Protestant evangelicals by putting more faith in the Bible and less faith in church tradition? Are Protestant evangelicals losing some of their faith in the Bible and becoming more like liberal Protestants and progressive Roman Catholics? How much disagreement is there over the Bible among Roman Catholics? Among evangelical Protestants? Is it enough to use words like "liberal" and "conservative" and "evangelical" nowadays? Or do we need to invent some new vocabulary?

And how does all this talk about the Bible affect my own use of the Bible? Do I stop believing it? Stop reading it? Stop preaching it? Or do I dig in my heels and refuse to recognize features of the Bible that I'd never seen before because they upset me, and upset some of what I thought the Bible meant? Or do I thank God for letting me see the Bible more accurately, and then cut it straighter, study it more avidly, believe it more faithfully, preach it more zealously with an open mind as well as an open heart?

We started with a prayer by the Roman Catholic artist Michelangelo. Let's close with the words of another Roman Catholic over two hundred years earlier, the literary artist Dante Alighieri, author of *The Divine Comedy*, not a prayer this time but a statement that Dante calls the "Origin of His Faith." He compares his Christian faith to a rare and precious jewel, asks where it came from, and then answers his own question in terms of the Holy Spirit's use of the Bible:

> Whence came this Jewel dear,
> From which doth every other virtue flow?
> . . . The Spirit's most abundant shower,
> Poured out upon the Pages New and Old

Hath of itself a syllogistic power
And hath convinced me with a strength so full,
That in comparison with it, I hold
Each other demonstration weak and dull.

Diversity in
New Testament Christology

*~ Delivered at a meeting of the
Phi Kappa Phi Honor Society ~*

The biblical theology movement of the mid-twentieth century emphasized the unity of the Bible, as in Harold Rowley's book, titled with that very phrase, and in A. M. Hunter's *The Unity of the New Testament*. A disintegration of the biblical theology movement and its emphasis went hand in hand with the rise of postmodernism and its emphasis on diversity among communities of faith. Strenuous efforts have been mounted here and there, if not to recapture unity, at least to trace a common thread running through the Bible and, especially for us Christians, through the New Testament, above all with regard to the doctrine of Christ. One thinks, for example, of J. D. G. Dunn's *Unity and Diversity in the New Testament*.

I suspect, however, that in conservative evangelical circles we rush so quickly to the side of unity that the benefits of diversity tend to get lost on us. Our motive may be pure: to defend the faith once for all delivered to the saints—a theological benefit. But the effect can be deleterious, too: a praxeological loss. I mean that it is not enough to know what the Scriptures teach; we also need to discern what is appropriate and inappropriate to be said from them in any given situation. Do not preach eternal security to careless Christians; preach the danger of apostasy by false and deceived professors of the faith. And vice versa to conscientious Christians suffering for the faith and tempted to doubt. Without denying the unity of Scripture, therefore, though perhaps pushing that unity to a higher level of abstraction, I wish to stress what those of our theological stripe almost instinctively resist, namely, diversity in New Testament Christology.

Most Christians think that the New Testament teaches the heavenly preexistence of Jesus as the second person of the Trinity, his coming down to earth by way of the incarnation, the virginal conception and birth as the means of incarnation, Jesus' holy life, atoning death, and bodily resurrection, his ascension back to heaven from where he had come in the first place, his present session at the right hand of God the Father, and his future coming to raise the dead and judge the world in righteousness. Taken as a whole, the New Testament does indeed spell out such a christological narrative; and the ancient creeds of the church illustrate and fortify this understanding of New Testament teaching about Christ. Think of the old Roman creed, forerunner of the Apostles' Creed: "I believe in God the Father Almighty and in Christ Jesus, his only Son, our Lord, who was born of the Holy Spirit and Mary the Virgin, who under Pontius Pilate was crucified and buried; the third day he rose from the dead, ascended to the heavens, [and] sat down at God's right hand, from where he will come to judge the living and the dead . . . ."

According to the Westminster Confession, "The Son of God, the second person in the Trinity, being very and eternal God, of one substance, and equal with the Father, did, when the fullness of time was come, take upon him man's nature, with all the essential properties and common infirmities thereof, yet without sin, being conceived by the power of the Holy Ghost, in the womb of the Virgin Mary, of her substance . . . . [He] was crucified and died; was buried, and remained under the power of death, yet saw no corruption. On the third day he arose from the dead, with the same body in which he suffered; with which also he ascended into heaven, and there sitteth at the right hand of his Father, making intercession; and shall return to judge men and angels at the end of the world."

But simple honesty demands our facing the fact that Christians have put together these and similar creedal portraits of Jesus with bits and pieces gathered from different parts of the New Testament. It is a composite portrait never found at one location in the New Testament. Jesus' preexistence comes from here, his virgin birth from there, his ascension from elsewhere, and so on. Take the canonical Gospels, for example. Mark starts with Jesus' baptism and ends, so far as we have the original text, with Jesus' resurrection. Matthew starts with Jesus' genealogy and birth and ends with his appearance after the resurrection. Luke starts with the birth of John the Baptist as well as with that of Jesus and, following appearances of the risen Jesus, ends with the ascension. John the evangelist starts with Jesus' eternal preexistence (though not as the human being we call Jesus) and ends with appearances of the risen Jesus following his ascension.*

If we had only the Gospel of Mark, we would never know about Jesus' preexistence as the Word, about the incarnation, or about the virgin birth of Jesus; and we would know about his ascension only by the implication of his statement that he was going to sit at God's right hand and then come to earth with clouds and great glory. We would know that Jesus was God's Son at his baptism, but we would not know of any earlier divine sonship. If we had the Gospels of Matthew and Luke as well as of Mark, we would know that the divine sonship of Jesus dated back to his conception and birth, and we would know that his

* See the discussion below for an early ascension in John.

conception and birth were virginal; but we would not know that he came down from heaven as preexistent deity to be conceived and born of the Virgin Mary. For all we would know, he started to exist at his virginal conception and birth. In fact, we would naturally assume so.

If we had the Gospel of Mark alone, we would think that Jesus was God's Son only because the Holy Spirit entered him at his baptism. If we had the Gospel of Matthew alone, we would think that Jesus was God's Son because of a unique action taken by the Holy Spirit on the Virgin Mary—this in fulfillment of Old Testament prophecy (Matthew 1:20–23 [compare Isaiah 7:14]). If we had only the Gospel of Luke and its companion volume, the Acts of the Apostles, we would think of Jesus as God's Son because the virgin birth represents, not a unique work of the Holy Spirit, but a divine generation like that of Adam, father of the human race. For Luke traces the genealogy of Jesus God's son back to Adam, whom he also calls God's son (Luke 3:38), and quotes Paul as saying on Mars' Hill that God made every nation of human beings from this one (apparently Adam, God's son), so that all of us human beings are God's offspring, God's generation (note well: generation, not creation), in accordance with the statement of Greek poets such as Aratus, whom Paul quotes: "as also some of your own poets have said, 'For also we are his offspring [Greek: *genos*, from which we get the English word "generation"]'" (Acts 17:26, 28–29).

Aratus, a Cilician, lived c. 315–240 B.C. Before him, Plato had alluded ironically to even earlier human beings who, doubtless knowing well their own ancestors (*progonous*, "progenitors"), declared themselves the descendants (*ekgonous*) of gods (*Timaeus* 40D). And Dio Chrysostom of Prusa, a youth during Paul's apostolic ministry, referred to the universally recognized and innately known truth of God's kinship (*xyngeneian*, "family relationship" or, more literally, "cogeneration") with the human race, so that we are "filled with the divine nature" and God is our "forefather" (*propatoros—Discourse* 12.27–28). Conversely, Dio also speaks of the kinship (*syngeneian*) of human beings with the gods (*Discourse* 12.61). Furthermore, Zeus and the other gods love human beings as being the gods' relatives (*xyngeneis*) because human beings are the offspring (*genos*, generation) of the gods, not of the Titans or of the Giants (other figures in Greek mythology). At some expense to the doctrine of creation, in other words, Luke-Acts assimilates the Christology of divine sonship to the old, continuing, and widespread Greek notion of the divine generation of the whole human race, so that Jesus' divine sonship becomes the example par excellence of all our divine sonship.

Of the four canonical Gospels, only that of John would give us reason to believe in Jesus as God's Son because he preexisted as divine. But John would give us no reason to believe that the preexistent Son of God became incarnate through the Virgin Mary; for not only does John omit the virgin birth. He also lets stand two references to Jesus as the son of Joseph (1:45; 6:42). Even though these references may represent characteristically Johannine irony, the irony need not imply the virgin birth, only that unbelievers knew Jesus as the son of Joseph without knowing him as much more importantly the Son of God.

Spatially, the narratives in Mark and Matthew start and end with Jesus on earth, though there is a reference to his being in heaven later on and coming from heaven back to earth. The narrative in Luke likewise starts with Jesus on earth, but ends with his ascension to heaven. Only John speaks about a down-and-up: Jesus comes down from heaven, walks on earth for a while, and goes back up to heaven, though in John he goes back up on Easter Day, not forty days later as in Luke-Acts; and then in John he commutes back from heaven to earth to make two or three further appearances on earth, whereas in Luke-Acts the risen Jesus stays on earth for forty days to make his appearances before ascending to heaven.

I know I have made an inference here, but hardly a greater one than the inferring of Jesus' ascension in Matthew and Mark from the prediction of his second coming: (1) John 7:37–39 says that the Spirit was not yet [*sc.* given] because Jesus was not yet glorified. (2) His glorification included his heavenly exaltation following the earthly ministry (see John 17:5, for example: "And now you, Father, glorify me alongside yourself with the glory that I had alongside you before the world existed"). (3) Yet Jesus bestowed the Spirit already on the evening of the first Easter Sunday (John 20:22). (4) Furthermore, on the first Easter Sunday morning Jesus told Mary Magdalene to stop touching him, because he had not yet ascended to the Father, and ordered her to go tell his disciples that he was ascending to his and their Father and God (John 20:17); (5) yet a week later Jesus invited Thomas to touch him (John 20:26–27). (6) So according to John, Jesus must have ascended in the meantime, indeed, between the command in the morning that Mary stop touching him and the bestowal of the Spirit that very evening.

We find the down-and-up of preexistence, incarnation, and exaltation back to heaven also in Paul's letters. But like John, he says nothing about a virgin birth as the means of incarnation. If we had only his letters, we would assume that God united his deity with a Jesus born naturally of two human parents, not supernaturally by an action of the Holy Spirit on the Virgin Mary. The author of Hebrews says that all things came into being both for Christ and through Christ and that Christ partook of our flesh and blood. So Hebrews, too, teaches the preexistence and incarnation of Jesus, but not his virgin birth. This is not to say that John, Paul, and the author of Hebrews denied the virgin birth, or would have denied it had they known about it; only that they did not know about it or, if they did know about it, that they ignored it despite their speaking about the incarnation. And in this connection, Hebrews' development of the incarnation into a portrait of Jesus as our great high priest has nothing quite like it in the rest of the New Testament.

Right among the Gospels we should note another difference, a huge one: In Mark, Matthew, and Luke, Jesus proclaims the kingdom of God. He does not proclaim himself. Except for the more mystifying than clarifying phrase "Son of Man," he does not even identify himself, at least not till Passion Week. When he calls himself the Son in relation to God his Father, he appears to be praying to God or meditating to himself, not identifying himself to his disciples, much less to the multitudes: "At that time Jesus answered and said, 'I praise you, Father, Lord of heaven and earth . . . . Yes, Father . . . . All things have been given over to me by my Father; and no one knows the Son except the Father; neither does anyone know the Father except the Son and the one to whom the Son wishes to reveal him" (Matthew 11:27–28 [compare Luke 10:21–22]). When in Mark and Luke, Peter identifies Jesus as the Christ, Jesus does not even acknowledge the identification, but merely tells the disciples (they are the only ones present) not to speak about him, and then he goes on to predict his death and resurrection as the Son of Man, not as the Christ (Mark 8:27–31; Luke 9:18–22). Later, he delivers a glancing reference to the disciples' belonging to Christ (Mark 9:41), but he does not acknowledge his christhood and divine sonship outright till the eve of his crucifixion, when standing trial before the Sanhedrin in Jerusalem (Mark 14:61–62).

In Matthew 16:13–20 Jesus describes Peter's confession as deriving from a divine revelation to Peter; but Jesus still commands the disciples not to tell anyone that he is the Christ, nor does he himself tell anyone. And when standing trial before the Sanhedrin in Matthew, he does not answer, "I am," to the high priest's question whether he is the Christ, the Son of God, as he does answer in Mark. Instead, he says, "*You* have said [that I am]" (Matthew 26: 63–64). Why does he not say, "I am," as in Mark? Because the high priest has put Jesus under oath ("I adjure you," the high priest has said), as he has *not* done in Mark's account; and Matthew will not let Jesus violate his own teaching against oaths by making an oathful self-declaration of his christhood and divine sonship. We find Jesus' teaching against oaths, not in Mark, but in Matthew 5:33–37 (compare James 5:12). So ethics swallows up Christology by making Jesus say less about himself in Matthew than he does in Mark. In Luke 22:66–71 he refuses to tell the Sanhedrin whether he is the Christ, and says that the identification of him as the Son of God belongs to their question, not to anything he has said.

In John, however, this proclaimer of God's kingdom turns into a proclaimer of himself. Jesus does not merely acknowledge his special identity. He advertises it. He does not limit the audience of this advertisement to his disciples. He advertises his identity to the multitudes. He does not wait till late in his ministry to launch his campaign of self-advertisement. He starts right away. Though he uses the standard terms "Christ" and "Son of God," by no means does he confine his self-identification to these terms. (In Jewish usage a messianic application of the phrase "Son of God" did not connote deity.) Rather, the Jesus of John heaps on himself one high-sounding designation after another: the one on whom the angels of God ascend and descend to and from the open heaven, that is, Jacob's ladder (1:51), the one who himself has descended from heaven and ascended to it (3:13), the giver of eternal life, the resurrection and the life, judge of the whole human race, bread of life, light of the world, I AM, good shepherd, he who is one with the Father, making himself equal with God, the way, the truth, and the life, the one who raises himself as well as everybody else from the dead.

And in addition to all these self-advertisements by Jesus, John has others recognize and advertise Jesus' identity, again from the very start, beginning with the Baptist's double declaration, "Behold, the Lamb of God!" (1:29, 36). The Baptist even testifies to Jesus' preexistence: "The one who is coming after me ranks ahead of me because he existed before me" (1:15). This advertisement of Jesus' identity by others continues in chapter 1 with the first disciples' declarations, already on the occasion of their becoming disciples, that Jesus is not only a rabbi, a teacher, but also the Messiah, the one about whom Moses wrote in the Law, and also the Prophets, the Son of God, and the King of Israel—a veritable laundry list of honorific designations straightaway in the first chapter of John's Gospel. No waiting till the middle of Jesus' ministry, as in Mark, Matthew, and Luke. In fact, from the very first sign which Jesus performs in John, the turning of water to wine at Cana of Galilee—from that very first sign onward he is making public revelation of his glory as the incarnate Word who was with God in the beginning and was God (2:11: "This beginning of signs Jesus performed in Cana of Galilee and manifested his glory, and his disciples believed in him" [compare 1:1, 14; 9:3; 11:4, 40]).

Since Jesus does not proclaim himself in Mark, Matthew, and Luke, he does not tell anybody to believe in him. Instead, he tells people to believe in the gospel of God, that is, in the good news that God's rule has come near (Mark 1:14–15: "Jesus came into Galilee preaching the gospel of God and saying, 'The time is fulfilled and the rule of God has come near; believe in the gospel'"). Jesus does refer in Mark 9:42; Matthew 18:6 to little ones who believe in him, but even that reference does not constitute a *call* to believe in him. On the other hand, since Jesus proclaims himself all over the map in John's Gospel, there Jesus repeatedly tells people of the necessity to believe in him if they are to have eternal life: "[the crowd] said to him, 'What should we do that we might work the works of God?' Jesus answered and said to them, 'This is the work of God, that you believe in him whom that one has sent'" (6:29); "for this is the will of my Father, that everyone who sees the Son and believes in him should have eternal life" (6:40); "for if you do not believe that I AM [note the divine title (compare Exodus 3:14 and John 8:58)], you will die in your sins" (8:24); "the one who believes in me will live even though that one dies, and everyone who is living and believes in me will never die" (11:25–26); "you believe in God, believe also in me" (14:1); and so on (see also 6:35; 7:38; 9:35–38; 10:38; 11:28; 12:44, 46; 13:19; 14:10–11; 16:30–31).

So a close look at New Testament Christology exposes what might seem to many Christians an astonishing diversity. Now Paul said that he became all things to all people that by all means he might save some (1 Corinthians 9:19–23). We might say that the authors of the New Testament made Jesus all things to all people that by all means *he* might save some. Because of persecution coming from the Roman Caesars, or about to come from them, the book of Revelation portrays Jesus as a conquering hero, riding a warhorse, the Lion of Judah, and also a lamb, but one with seven horns with which at his return he will gore the persecutors of his people. Matthew's church is suffering persecution, too, but not from the Roman Caesars; rather, from Jewish synagogues. So he portrays Jesus as meek and mild, riding humbly on a donkey, a model of non-retaliation in accordance with his own teaching in the Sermon on the Mount (Matthew 5–7). The superpower of the Caesars made it useless to attempt retaliation against them; so Revelation could only give a militant hope for the future. But retaliation against the synagogues might seem feasible right now; so Matthew portrays Jesus, not in the way of Revelation, which might incite retaliation, but quite oppositely in a way designed to counteract the temptation to retaliate.

As we all know, the particular circumstances in and for which Paul wrote differ from one letter to another, but in general he wrote as the apostle to Gentiles to predominantly Gentile Christians, whose background included pagan cults such as the mystery religions that featured a divine lord. So Paul presents Jesus as Lord of the Christian cult ("cult" in its technical sense of a system for worshiping a deity). To this end, Paul concentrates on Jesus' death, resurrection, and exaltation and pays almost no attention to the Christology of Jesus' earthly ministry, and very little to that of Jesus' preexistence and incarnation. After all, the lords of the pagan cults, over against whom Paul puts Jesus (1 Corinthians 8:5–6: "For . . . just as there are . . . many lords, yet for us there is . . . one Lord, Jesus Christ")—these lords of the pagan cults did not become human beings to lead earthly lives that could have elicited very much interest from Paul in Jesus' preexistence, incarnation, and earthly ministry. But the mythology concerning those pagan lords did include their death and revival in the underworld. The Jesus of Paul goes one better by rising bodily from the dead and enjoying exaltation in heaven.

On the other hand, Luke writes for an audience of sophisticated Gentiles, like the "most excellent Theophilus" whom he addresses, apparently God-fearers, high-minded people distrustful of polytheism and more interested in human beings than in cultic deities, more interested in humanity than in divinity. So Luke humanizes the divinity of Jesus by drawing a parallel between the divine sonship of Jesus and the divine sonship of Adam, and thus derivatively the divine sonship of the whole human race. He ascribes to Jesus an ideal human development: "Jesus advanced in wisdom and stature and in favor with God and human beings" (Luke 2:52); that is to say, he grew intellectually, physically, spiritually, and socially—a full-orbed human development such as would have drawn admiration even in the gymnasium at Athens. He displayed precocity at the age of twelve when in the temple he amazed scholars with his understanding and answers—a child prodigy. As an adult, he embodied the loftiest ideals of human being. He exhibited great breadth of human sympathy—for tax collectors and sinners, Samaritans, women, widows—yet moved easily among the high and mighty and wealthy. The Jesus of Luke is cosmopolitan, attractive, approachable, convivial, the kind we would like to eat dinner with and then tarry at table for conversation and drinks till midnight, as in fact people do with Jesus in Luke.

The circumstances of John's writing differed radically. He wrote—I think it has been established well enough, though some scholars entertain reservations—John wrote during the rising tide of Gnosticism, which denied the humanity of Christ either by making the incarnation only apparent (docetism) or by distinguishing a divine spirit, Christ, from a human being, Jesus, and saying that the divine spirit came on the human being not till the human's baptism and left before the crucifixion (Cerinthianism). Yet other Gnostics, called Simonians, said that Simon of Cyrene not only carried Jesus' cross but also died on it in place of Jesus.

So John emphasizes the deity of the human Jesus. The Word who was God became flesh. The glory of the human Jesus was that of the only, the *unique* Son of God. (Notice the difference from Luke's Christology of *shared* divinity.) There is only one person Jesus Christ, not Jesus and Christ; and that one person came in water and in blood according to 1 John 5:6, not in water only (apparently baptism by John the Baptist). According to John the evangelist, the Baptist testified that the Spirit which came on Jesus at the first (I say "at the first" because the Fourth Gospel does not mention Jesus' baptism), the Spirit stayed on him, did not leave him later, as taught by the Cerinthians, so that Jesus' death is described, not as an expiration, as in Mark 15:37 and Luke 23:46 (*exepneusen*), nor as a relinquishment of his human spirit, as in Matthew 27:50 (*aphêken to pneuma*), but as a giving over of the Spirit (capital S: *paredôken to pneuma*—John 19:30). Now that he had been glorified by being lifted up on the cross he could start giving over the Spirit in accordance with

John 7:37–39. Thus, right after his death and further glorification by resurrection and ascension Jesus could breathe on the disciples and say, "Receive the Holy Spirit" (20:22). He came, not in water only, but in water and in blood: he really died, as shown in John's Gospel by the outflow of blood and water at the piercing of Jesus' side. And he carried his cross "by himself" (19:17). Simon did not carry it for him, as in Matthew, Mark, and Luke; much less did Simon die on the cross in Jesus' place.

Like John, Hebrews also stresses incarnational Christology, but in quite different circumstances and therefore with a different twist. Not Gnosticism, with its intellectual snobbery, but Judaism, with its sacerdotal (priestly) tradition, offers the backdrop against which to understand the Christology of Hebrews. Jewish priests officiated at the offering of animals in blood-sacrifice to atone for sins. But Jesus could not have officiated at such sacrifices if he had wanted to. He belonged to the wrong tribe and family, the tribe of Judah and the family of David within that tribe. Jewish priests had to belong to the tribe of Levi and the family of Aaron within it. So the author of Hebrews has Jesus officiate over a better sacrifice, that of himself. But to do so, Jesus had to have a body of flesh and blood (Hebrews 2:14–17). Hence, the emphasis on incarnation, but not incarnation as a means of divine revelation, as in the Gospel of John, so much as incarnation as a means toward human sacrifice.

To tease out this difference a little more, through the incarnation in John deity *reveals* itself to humanity by taking the form of a human being. Through the incarnation in Hebrews, deity *learns* humanity by taking the form of a human being: "he learned obedience through what he suffered" (Hebrews 5:8b); "in every respect he was tempted as we are" (Hebrews 4:15); "and having been perfected [we never find a phrase like that in John, where it is the disciples, not the divine Word, who need to be perfected (John 17:23)], he became the source of eternal salvation for all who obey him, having been designated by God a high priest according to the order of Melchizedek" (Hebrews 5:9–10). Jesus the divine Word in John is not tempted. The stories of Jesus' temptation appear only in Mark, Matthew, and Luke.

Nor does the Jesus of John have to learn obedience through suffering. He does not even suffer, at least not as a victim. He prays self-composedly for his disciples (John 17) instead of throwing himself on the ground in a sweat of emotional turmoil and praying about his own fate. How else would we expect God in the flesh to behave than with self-composure? Not only is there no agony in Gethsemane. At the cross there is no prayer on behalf of Jesus' crucifiers, "Father, forgive them; for they know not what they do," because although Pontius Pilate gives Jesus over to the Jews and they crucify him (19:16–18), at a profounder level the Jesus of John puts *himself* on the cross ("No one takes my life from me; rather, I lay it down of my own accord" [10:18]). He practically insists on his arrest: he goes out to meet the band who would take him, and has to ask them twice whom they seek, and identifies himself twice as the object of their search; and he even lays down a condition under which they can take him ("If then you are looking for me, let these [disciples] go away" [18:2–8]). John quotes him as saying on the cross, "I thirst," but introduces the statement as a fulfilment of Scripture, not as a sign of suffering. And so, ever in control, the incarnate Word of God dies by his own volition after announcing that his works are finished: "knowing that all things [which things presumably refer to 'the works' the Father had given him to do] were already finished . . . . he said, 'They are finished' [not '*It* is finished,' but the 'all things,' 'the works']" (19:28, 30).*

New Testament Christology exhibits diversity, then, a diversity prompted by varying circumstances—political, social, economic, ethnic, educational, religious. To say so is not to say that New Testament Christologies were wholly determined by such circumstances, as though the figure of Christ was made of Silly Putty which the New Testament authors molded into whatever shape they thought was required by their varying circumstances. Certain brute facts about Jesus provided both a skeleton with which to work and parameters within which to work. Nevertheless, my emphasis has fallen on differences in New Testament Christology, so much so that a moment ago the plural slipped in: New Testament Christologies. Different parts of the New Testament give us different Christologies—not completely different from one another, to be sure, but strikingly different, sometimes disconcertingly different, and certainly far more different from one another than has usually been thought in the church at large.

But, you might say, we now have all the New Testament. So what does it matter whether Paul and Mark say nothing about the virgin birth, whether Mark, Matthew, and Luke say nothing about Jesus' preexistence, whether Luke's and John's notions of Jesus' divine sonship differ from each other as broadly humanistic and narrowly sectarian, respectively, and so on. It matters because the diversity of New Testament Christology raises important interpretive and theological questions: Should we systematize the

*The Greek verb is singular, but Greek neuter plural subjects regularly take singular verbs.

Christologies of Matthew, Mark, Luke, and John, of Paul, Hebrews, James, Peter, and Jude, so as to produce an overarching, comprehensive, single new Testament Christology? Or should we let the New Testament authors speak individually about Jesus, as they originally did? To use hackneyed metaphors, is New Testament Christology a melting pot or a mixing bowl? A soup in which different ingredients are pureed together, or a salad in which they do not lose their individual identity? Does the canonization of books called the New Testament mean that we should interpret them by each other so as to get a unified view of Jesus? Or does the New Testament canon present us with a range of different Christologies any one of which is acceptable by itself?

Are Paul and Mark and John less Christian because they seem not to know about, and therefore not to believe in, the virgin birth? Are Mark, Matthew, and Luke less Christian because they seem not to know about, and therefore not to believe in, the divine preexistence of Jesus? Or did these evangelists know about and believe in his divine preexistence and virgin birth but omit to mention them because these matters seemed irrelevant to their authorial purposes? Nowadays is a true Christian bound to accept all the Christologies of the New Testament even though it was once possible to be truly Christian on the acceptance of only a single, incomprehensive Christology? Or might a contemporary person become a Christian and stay one by accepting, say, Luke's Christology without accepting, perhaps even while rejecting, the Christologies of Paul, Mark, and John? In the case of rejection, I do not think so; but the question is worth discussing. Do New Testament Christologies complement each other or compete with each other? For example, does Luke's upwardly mobile humanistic Christology, a man rising to the level of God, undermine John's downwardly mobile theological Christology, God descending to the level of a man? Or do they fill out a harmonious picture?

Does the New Testament canon limit the range of acceptable Christologies, or provide us with paradigms for the development of new Christologies better suited than old ones to modern concerns? Does the New Testament tell us *what* to do, or *how* to do it? What does the culture of modern psychology have to say about a contemporary Christian portrait of Jesus? What do *different* schools of modern psychology have to say about contemporary portraiture of Jesus? What would sociological portraits of him look like? Sociobiological portraits? Should the human genome project affect our understanding and presentation of Jesus?

Should we be developing different Christologies for blacks? For whites? For Asians? For Hispanics? For the urban poor? For the rural poor? For the suburban middle class? For Wall Street? For Main Street? For men? For women? For children? Where do we stop? Can we stop? Should we start? Or have we been developing such Christologies all along, more or less unaware of what we were doing? How would new Christologies differ from one another? What thread might connect them together? How thick a thread would be required to keep them from unraveling into different religions? Or would it be wrongheaded to suit different Christologies to diverse needs in society? Should Christology provide common ground on which to stand? Should it erase our cultural differences, or at least overarch them, rather than catering to them? Would the development of new Christologies contribute to the spread of the gospel, or would it expose the gospel to heresy, the New Testament having presented models to be satisfied with, not models to be imitated? Are New Testament Christologies sufficient or seminal? How should we regard the diversity of New Testament Christology, and the fundamental questions generated by this phenomenon? As off-limits, troubling, unsettling, unspeakable, and dangerous to the life and limb of Christian orthodoxy? Or as inviting, urgent, and essential to the revitalization of Christian orthodoxy in an ever-changing world? I have my answers to these questions, rather conservative ones, as it happens; but all of us—you, too—need to reach for responsible answers. Often the line between sufficient and seminal is fuzzy, for example.

A while back I made a crude reference to Silly Putty. I would like to close with a cultivated but otherwise similar reference to an ancient Greek myth. In his *Odyssey* 4. 382–569 Homer tells about the old man of the sea, Proteus, an Egyptian god who knows the depths and paths of every sea, so that he can give unerring advice to any seafarer facing the untold dangers of a voyage. The trouble is, Proteus does not like to give such advice. You have to grab him, hold him tight, and then force it out of him with questions. But it is hard to hold him tight, because when you do grab him, he tries to slip out of your grasp by changing from one shape to another, as when in the *Odyssey* Menelaus and his men grabbed him. At first Proteus turned into a bearded lion, then into a serpent, then into a leopard, then into a huge boar, then into flowing water, and finally into a tall, leafy tree. Try as he would, however, Proteus could not slip from the grasp of Menelaus and his men; and so, having grown tired and weary from the effort, he answered the questions of Menelaus concerning a homeward voyage.

One might say that like Proteus, the diverse Christ of the New Testament takes many shapes and forms. There is a difference, of course: Proteus assumed many shapes and forms to avoid answering people's questions, whereas the Christ of the New Testament assumes many shapes and forms to answer questions. But that difference only highlights the initiative of divine grace. The issue remains: Does Christ still take many shapes and forms? Or does the closing of the New Testament canon mean that like Proteus, Christ is—so to speak—tired of assuming different shapes and forms, that he has assumed all the shapes and forms he needs to have assumed for answering our questions? In his canonical diversity is he able without further metamorphoses to answer the fundamental questions that grow out of modern psychology, sociology, sociobiology, the human genome project, the black experience, the white experience, the Hispanic and Asian experiences, women's experiences, men's experiences? Or do these disciplines and experiences call for new Christologies patterned after but not limited to the old Christologies of the New Testament? I leave the question to you, but with one added observation, a feature of the Protean myth that I omitted. Before the weary old man of the sea would finally answer the questions of Menelaus, he subjected Menelaus to some questioning of his own. Likewise, the Christ of the New Testament insists on questioning us before answering us. What that might mean I also leave to you.

Shall We Dance?

*~ Delivered in response to Professor Marianne Robins'
Phi Kappa Phi Lecture,*

*"Body Building: Dancing, Decadence and Decay
in Early-Modern France" ~*

*(Readers can infer from this response the contents of
Professor Robins' lecture.)*

Your lecture, Professor Robins, opened with a quotation of
Saint Ephrem, a Syrian church father of the fourth century:

> The art of dancing itself sprang from the mouth of
> the Old Serpent, and not from any human hand.
> The same Serpent that taught us fornication and
> idolatry, also taught us how to dance. Dance is a
> ring with the Devil at its center and fallen angels on
> its circumference. One cannot both serve God and
> dance with the devils.

In that quotation I thought I heard my father's voice crying
out from the grave. He was a Baptist pastor and proud to
identify himself as a fundamentalist. One day a
telemarketer for the Arthur Murray Dance Studios called
our home. My father picked up the phone. The
telemarketer offered him some dance lessons if he could
answer a question. My father shot back, "I'd rather sing for
the Lord than dance for the Devil," and hung up.
Ironically, he was nearly tone-deaf. Later, I considered it a
judgment from God, at my father's behest, when after
taking several lessons in square-dancing I was dancing in
our gymnasium with the granddaughter of the founder of
Fuller Theological Seminary and stepped on the hem of
her floor-length dress so that it ripped apart at the waistline
and threatened to fall off. She beat a hasty retreat, and I
reformed.

My congratulations to you, Professor Robins, now also a doctor, on a very informative as well as entertaining lecture. You've drawn on history, sociology, art, and religion; and you've related them to each other in a way that exhibits the educational ideals of Westmont as a Christian liberal arts college. Thank you.

For me, the best lectures are the ones that incite the most questions. By that standard your lecture succeeds brilliantly. My questions will betray my ignorance, but the first one has to do with *your* ignorance. You claim to know little about the actual practice of dancing in early modern France, and about the significance of dancing to the dancers themselves. Yet you describe the dances as taking place in cemeteries; as organized and done mainly though not exclusively by young people, prominently by students; as often organized by fraternities; as open to the public; as funded by public donations; as accompanied by paid musicians; as including leaping, jumping, back-slapping, and crushing handshakes; and as often lasting all night. You also understand the dances as means of match-making, as both building and challenging communal order, and as intimately associated with death and the dead as well as with life and the living. My goodness but you're an ambitious scholar! What's there left to know? Can you tell us your *un*answered questions about dance in early modern France?

Your title, "Body-Building," plays on the double effect of dance as an exercise that builds the individual physical body and as an interpersonal activity that builds the social body. These effects look good, but opposition came from religious reformers, particularly males. Do we have evidence of any female opposition? If so, did that opposition arise out of the same concerns that drove male opponents? If out of different concerns, what were they? If we don't have any evidence of female opposition, why don't we?

Did the religious reformers include lay people as well as clergy? The opposition grew out of concern for sexual morality, but also out of concern that dancing took match-making away from parents. Was this latter kind of opposition limited to the upper classes, because only there would parents be concerned that their children not marry into a lower class? Did the concern for class distinctions arise only at the end of the early modern period? If so, why not earlier? And did the clergy who opposed dancing do so out of concern for class distinctions as well as sexual morality? Or are we dealing with two different streams of opposition, one clerical, the other lay, one religiously moral, the other secularly social?

You've told us that married adults danced, though not so much as the unmarried youth. Was adult dancing opposed, too? If not, why not? If so, on what grounds? The adults were already married, so that presumably the question of class was passé. Did the religious reformers fear that dancing would lead to sexual infidelity on the part of married people?

Because of short life expectancy and a high rate of infant mortality, you say that "physical beauty held less attraction than endurance and a sturdy constitution." What then do we make of Canon Arbeau's statement? Don't its references to shapeliness, odor, and such like support the criterion of beauty even among the lower classes? Arbeau does say that dancing exhibits good health and sound limb, and such were necessary for marriage—but not sufficient. For after dancing, he says, and beyond the exhibition of good health and sound limb came kissing and fondling to ascertain shapeliness and odor. It was good kissing and good fondling, then, not good dancing, that led to marriage. Good dancing passed the physical test, but didn't provide the main attraction to marriage. Beauty did. Or have I misread Arbeau?

Being on the side of Apollo, the god of order, and against Dionysus, the god of disorder, clergy wanted to keep young people from sexual and other misbehavior. Lay people wanted them to "get it out of their system." Are you implying that we, too, should encourage our young people to get sexual and other misbehavior out of their system by engaging in it before they marry and settle down? Or could one argue to the contrary that what you call the relatively undisciplined behavior of adults in early modern France shows the failure of dancing to get it out of young people's system, perhaps that dancing encouraged habits of misbehavior that extended into adulthood? And does it really matter that "the sexual depravity of dancers was already, by the 16th century, an old argument, and that it would age even further right down to fairly recent days"? Why should age decrease the validity of an argument? Might not someone else appeal at least as validly to "the wisdom of the ages"?

Your positing an inner connection between dancing and hostility, either by way of ritual expression or by way of actual rebellion, raises a question. In none of the examples you cited is dancing as such an act of hostility. It wasn't the display of virility in a dance that produced violence, but the mockery of that display which did. It wasn't dancing together by the inhabitants of one village that insulted the inhabitants of another village; it was the invasion of the other villagers' space. It wasn't anything inherent in dancing that made it rebellious against a local lord; it was his prohibition that made the dancing rebellious. So in contrast with the relation between dancing and sexual misconduct, wasn't the relation between dancing and hostility more adventitious than organic?

Do I hear in your discussion echoes of Nietzsche's "will to power" and Foucault's "rhetoric of power": life is a never-ending competition for power, for dominance? You're not satisfied with moral concern as the sole reason for religious opposition to dance. To support a desire for dominance as an additional reason, you say, "It is therefore difficult to argue that opponents of dance simply wanted to impose a semblance of moral order." Your "therefore" refers back to two observations: first, that the moral argument was used against upper class dancing as well as against lower class dancing. But that fact doesn't require an additional reason for the opposition to dancing, does it? Doesn't it show only that dancing was considered morally dangerous whoever did the dancing, lower class or upper class? Here's the second observation behind your "therefore": by the late 1600s many of the upper class "had adopted the kind of restrained bodily and social behavior we now associate with gentility and refinement." But what about the late 1400s through the early 1600s, the vast bulk of the early modern period, before upper class adoption of a genteel, refined behavior? And did the later gentility and refinement in dancing demonstrably curtail sexual misbehavior? If not, why couldn't the religious opponents of dance have continued their opposition into the late 1600s simply out of concern for moral order in upper as well as lower classes, not additionally out of an elemental desire for dominance? And despite Arbeau's support of dancing as essential to a well-ordered society, doesn't the detail he provides about kissing, touching, savoring, smelling, and ascertaining of shapeliness, all of which ensued from dancing, favor the guardians of sexual morality?

If more than a moral concern is needed, though, why not consider the theory that opposition to dance may have stemmed also from a carry-over of medieval Christian asceticism, an almost Manichean view of the physical body as inherently evil, so that its appetites need suppressing as much as possible? And why not consider the opposition as also growing out of resentment toward sex because of its wild, overpowering force as when even as a Christian, Saint Augustine complained to God that his genitals seemed to lead a life of their own, independent of his will, or as when Westmont men periodically complain to their student newspaper, *The Horizon*, that the provocative dress of some Westmont women makes it practically impossible to maintain purity of mind and matter? You admit that "dancing encouraged explicit displays of sexual prowess." So don't these historical and psychobiological theories deserve as much consideration as the sociological theory of a contest over who gets to dominate the culture?

In your theory of such a contest you seem to prefer domination by lay people because their encouragement of dance "lent prominent roles to women" as well as to "the community's youth." You've spoken of mothers' and young women's prominent roles only in connection with the upper classes, however, whereas you're concentrating on the lower classes, and not for sure even among the upper classes until the 17th and 18th centuries, largely past the early modern period of your topic. And so far as I can tell, what you call the alternative "moral order" fostered by dancing gave young men and their fathers dominance over women. The traditional codes of honor that laymen enforced had to do with keeping outsiders from stealing their sexual property, the young women of their village. But that kind of code seems to have aimed for social cohesion more than for a morality alternative to that of the religious reformers. Instead of talking about "competing moral standards," then, wouldn't it be truer to talk about competition between a religious standard, designed to preserve sexual morality, and a social standard, designed to defend the sexual property of males even at the frequent expense of the sexual immorality admittedly spurred by dance? In other words, wouldn't it be more accurate to talk about early modern French dancing in terms of the dominance of men over women?

You say that "dancing challenged social and sexual segregation" and "brought the individual into community." But at what cost? You described the dancing as an athletic exercise so strenuous that it weeded out the unhealthy and unsound of limb as unfit for marriage and procreation. Doesn't your communitarian defense of dance come then at the cost of a sociobiological Darwinism, survival of the fittest: only the fittest chose each other to procreate offspring? Pity the weak; dancing made them social outcasts.

Ah, you say, but there's one dance that integrated everybody, excluded nobody: the dance of death. Although some depictions of that dance portrayed the dancers as a group, however, other depictions portrayed them in separate vignettes. So even the dance of death didn't always or necessarily produce social integration. And how do you reconcile your statement that "death united all in that last grand round dance, the dance of death" with your statement that "the dance of death . . . served as a conspicuous ritual display of status and importance, and promoted the ideal of a sharply-ordered society," that is, a society carved up into hierarchical ranks?

Finally, I'm puzzled by the association of death with dancing by young people. I know that the process of dying puts one in a liminal state between life and death, and that young people occupy the liminal space between childhood and adulthood. But these are very different kinds of liminality, aren't they? The very athleticism of young people's dancing belies the connotation of death, doesn't it? Their kind of dancing is for the healthy and lively, isn't it?

You've tried to help me out of my puzzle by saying that lame people were commonly believed to act as intermediaries between the living and the dead, and then by rationalizing the activity of young people as intermediaries between the living and the dead because young people are "limping by nature (one foot in childhood, one in adulthood)." But is this comparison of young people to lame people yours, or something we find in literature of the period? If it's only yours, how does it help me understand the rationale of early modern French people for associating death with young people's dancing? Besides, having one foot in childhood and one in adulthood makes me think of straddling rather than limping. And even if I should accept the figure of limping, I'm still stuck on the disagreement between limping and leaping.

Your paper illustrates the value and interest to be found in the study of history. Modesty kept you from making a more forceful pitch for your own discipline, which I think could help us commune with the dead better than dancing did. Please accept my questions as an equally modest attempt to invite responses that would make an already strong lecture even stronger. I summarize my many questions in a single question: "Shall we dance?" Intellectually, of course; I wouldn't want to damage your dress.

Well, Dad, right or wrong, I tried.

A Charge

~ Delivered to Dr. Tremper Longman III
on the occasion of his installation into the
Robert H. Gundry Chair of Biblical Studies,
Westmont College, October 22, 1999 ~

Professor Dr. Longman, I'm speaking to you, but you're sitting behind me. This is a gymnasium, though; so let's play as if the audience out there is a backboard off which I can bank my shots into your basket.

First, my hearty congratulations for the honor you've just received! It brings pleasure to me as it surely does to you. I'd like to go on in this vein, but my job here isn't so much to commend you as to command you. You claim to be an expert on the Bible, especially the Old Testament. Otherwise we wouldn't call you a professor. The very word "professor" refers to someone who makes a verbal claim. That's the "fess" part of "professor." But it's also a verbal claim made before other people. That's the "pro" part of "professor." A professor is somebody who makes a verbal claim before other people.

Since we've accepted the claim you've made before us, you've been given a chair. Question: Why a chair? Why not a lectern or a pulpit? Answer: Because sitting is the posture of authority that teachers take. Jesus said that the scribes and Pharisees sat on the chair of Moses. Every once in a while the pope speaks *ex cathedra*, "from the chair," and faithful Roman Catholics bow to his authority when he does. Our Lord himself—after reading out of the prophet Isaiah in the synagogue at Nazareth, he sat down to teach from the passage. And he sat down to teach his disciples the Sermon on the Mount. He took the posture of authority. Though your authority doesn't equal his, you've been given a chair in recognition of your authority as a scholar and teacher. And the fact that yours is an endowed chair, one that's funded by special gifts donated out of the generosity of benefactors—that fact heightens the honor bestowed on you. It shows you're being recognized as a scholar and teacher par excellence.

So my first charge is that you comport yourself with a dignity that suits this high honor, and with a seriousness that suits the authority of an academic chair. I don't mean you should shed the affability that immediately strikes everybody who meets you. Who'd want you to stop wearing Polo pullovers and start wearing starched shirts, the way somebody else I know does? But I do mean that mixed in with your affability there should be a gravitas that returns honor to the chair with which you've been honored. Gravitas, gravity, weight—as you know better than most of us, the Hebrew word for "honor" means "weight."

But I need to mention the weight of responsibility as well as the weight of honor. James the brother of Jesus says that not many of us should be teachers, because teachers will receive greater judgment than nonteachers will. James proceeds to warn against misusing the tongue, the primary instrument of teaching. Then he wraps up his charge by warning against boasting and selfish ambition, which he calls earthly and demonic, and by urging meekness and the wisdom that comes from above, which he describes as pure, peaceful, gentle, persuadable, and so on. If in the *final* final exam teachers who don't hold an endowed chair will be judged by these standards more strictly than their students, how much more strictly will the holder of an endowed chair be judged by these standards. You and I should be quivering in our robes right now. (They're laughing; I'm serious.)

Some years back my doctoral supervisor, Professor F. F. Bruce, whose many books populate our library and other libraries around the world—at the time he was president of the Society of New Testament Studies. We were meeting at the University of Aberdeen, Scotland, where as an undergraduate he'd studied the Greek and Latin classics and made such unbelievably good grades that on campus people were still talking about them thirty years later. He'd been elected president of the British Society of Old Testament Studies, too. He held the prestigious Rylands Chair of Biblical Criticism and Exegesis at Manchester University. Most outstandingly of all, he'd been elected a Fellow of the British Academy. A number of his former students gathered in a private home to honor him. One by one, we sang his praises. But when we'd finished, the first thing he said was, "It does no good to any man's soul to hear such nice things said about him." He wasn't unappreciative, just afraid—afraid of corruptive possibilities in the reception of honor.

No wonder, then, that Jesus, whose own chair is a throne at God's right hand, whose authority as a teacher totally eclipses ours, out of whose mouth come the very words of God by which we human beings are to live, for he is "Immanuel, 'God with us'"—in comparison with him, none of us is a teacher. We're all students. No wonder he told his disciples not to accept the title "Rabbi," which means "my Great One." Beside him I'm not great. You're not great. Nobody's great. Yet Jesus said, "Take my yoke upon you and learn from me, because I am meek and lowly in heart." Imagine! This great and exalted teacher, this divine teacher who sits in the most heavily endowed chair of all, endowed with his Father's heavenly glory—he is meek and lowly. Not meek and lowly just in outward appearance, either. "Meek and lowly in *heart*," in the way he thinks about himself.

If we do learn from Jesus, we'll not brag about our scholarly credentials. We won't boast of our academic accomplishments. We won't parade the books we've written. We won't take offense when people fail to call us "Professor" or "Doctor." And, I dare say, we won't list our degrees and titles behind our names unless it's necessary to enhance the reputation of the college rather than our own reputation, or to enhance the acceptance of our work rather than our persons. So my second charge to you, Professor Longman, is to guard against the arrogance into which scholarly success can suck any of us. Follow Jesus' example, and make yourself an example, an example of genuine humility.

Professor Bruce was only half right, though. Hearing nice things said about you is dangerous—true. But it's also encouraging, and encouragement is good. The granting of this chair now is a way of anticipating what Christ himself will say at the last convocation, the everlasting convocation: "Well done, good and faithful servant; enter into the joy of your Lord." As Nehemiah the wall-builder said, "The joy of the Lord is your strength." So let the joy of this occasion be, not only our joy in you, but also the Lord's joy in you; and let his joy in you combine with ours to strengthen you in building the walls of this Jerusalem, Westmont College, till Christ himself finishes building the jasper walls of that bright and shining city, the New Jerusalem, which is none other than the church, of which we are a part—his bride, adorned with the very glory of God and readied for the marriage supper of the Lamb. You're a co-worker with Christ. You're helping him build that wall right here on this campus. Your installation into an endowed chair acknowledges your work and aims to strengthen you with joy till you fulfill the ministry that God has given you. Take the joy, and translate it into strength for the work at hand.

There's one more item in my charge to you. Because of the honor bestowed on you, you're now in a better position to bestow honor on others, to share your honor with them. Take the honor you've received and distribute it to your colleagues on the faculty in the way you treat them, to administrators and other staffers who make it possible for you to do your work here, and also to the Board of Trustees. Distribute your honor to students, too. Show them courtesy. Respect their questions. Sympathize with them in their failures. Praise them in their successes. But don't—don't dishonor them by expecting less of them than they're capable of. You won't honor them by letting them get away with shoddy work, or little work. Jesus' yoke is easy and his burden light, not because he gives us easy assignments. Just read the Sermon on the Mount: "Except your righteousness surpasses that of the scribes and Pharisees, you will by no means enter the kingdom of heaven. . . . You shall be perfect as your heavenly Father is perfect." I've never given a homework assignment as demanding as that. You probably haven't, either. Someone has suggested that Jesus' yoke is easy and his burden light because he's in the other side of the yoke pulling the load with us, helping us. So also you, Professor Longman, don't delegate your work with students to others. You yourself get in the other side of the yoke that you lay on your students' shoulders, and pull along with them.

Finally, distribute the honor bestowed on you by throwing yourself, body and soul, into the life of the college at large. At some institutions endowed chairs are tickets to splendid isolation. The holders of those chairs can trot off and (as they say) "do their own thing." They're almost expected to absent themselves from campus activities and pursue their own agendas independently. Not so at Westmont. We're a residential college. Here an endowed chair isn't a ticket to splendid isolation. It's a command performance that calls you to share your knowledge and wisdom not only in the classroom, but also in the committee room, in faculty forums and business meetings, in dialogues during seminars and following special lectures. Your endowed chair calls for your presence at art exhibits, drama productions, concerts and recitals, and it asks you to participate in the receptions and discussions that often accompany such events.

What a long list! An impossible list! You'll have to be selective, of course. But your chairship does say to you, "You don't belong to yourself alone. You don't belong only to your department. You belong to the whole college." Look at this crowd in front of you. It's the college as a whole: trustees, administrators, faculty, staff, students, alumni and friends of the college. The whole institution is honoring you. You'll enlarge that honor, for yourself as well as for the rest of us, by returning it through self-involvement in the larger life of the college.

It used to be a practice in Christian families for parents to give their children on the verge of adulthood a life-verse out of the Bible, a verse that would serve as a guiding light. So I close my charge with the life-verse that was given to me. It comes from the Apostle Paul: "Therefore, whether you eat or drink, or whatever you do, do all to the glory of God."

Part Two:

Sermonic Talks

Be Perfect

~ Delivered in chapel with reference to Matthew 5:48: "You shall be perfect as your heavenly Father is perfect" ~

As you can see, I'm standing in for our chaplain. Last Monday he pointed to God's kingdom as the overarching message that Jesus proclaimed and taught. Later, Christians proclaimed Jesus; but he proclaimed the kingdom of God. And who is this God that brought his rule to earth in the activities of Jesus Christ? He's the Father, whom Jesus addressed—and whom he taught his disciples to address—as "Abba." Our chaplain pointed out that this is the Aramaic word which Jewish children learned in their cradles, something like our "Dadda" or "Daddy."

True, but don't draw a false conclusion. "Abba" is not entirely like "Daddy." "Abba" was what grown Jewish men continued to call their fathers. They never stopped calling their fathers "Abba." It was the only word they had for a father. They learned it when they were children, just as they learned many other words when they were children; but contrary to what you often hear, it was not a childish word.

And if we're talking about the Gospel of Matthew, as we are this morning, it's especially important to note that Matthew goes out of his way to avoid any childishness that you might pick up from "Abba." Not only doesn't he use "Abba" anywhere in his Gospel. Not only does he even eliminate "Abba" when he finds it in Mark's version of Jesus' prayer in the Garden of Gethsemane (compare Matthew 26:39 with Mark 14:36). But also, when Matthew writes the ordinary *Greek* word for a father in the Lord's Prayer, he adds "Our" and "who art in heaven": "Our Father, who art in heaven." Luke's version of the Lord's Prayer doesn't have either one of these additions; so

Matthew must be making a special point (compare Matthew 6:9 with Luke 11:2).

"Our" emphasizes that the Lord's Prayer is a communal prayer, a prayer to be prayed by a congregation of adults, not a prayer to be prayed individually as by a child to her Daddy. "Who art in heaven" stresses how high God is above us rather than how close he is to us on earth, as though he were a daddy bending over our cradle or cuddling us in his arms. Supremacy is in view—majesty, transcendence. And when, on the other hand, Jesus is quoted as saying that you should become like little children (Matthew 18:3–4), don't let modern western notions of children make you think of child-like faith in a father. Those were the days before youth culture. Children occupied the lowest rung on the social ladder. So to become like a child, as Jesus himself goes on to say, means to humble yourself by taking a lowly position in relation to others—as he did—not to be simple in your faith (as important as that may be in its own way).

All of which comes down to this point: Matthew writes his Gospel to foster grownup Christianity, not to perpetuate childish Christianity, not even a child-like Christianity in *our* sense of child-like. Matthew is about the business that *we*'re supposed to be about here at Westmont: transforming childish Christians into adult Christians, adolescent Christians into grownup Christians, high school Christians into collegiate Christians, Christians who know only enough to say "Daddy" into Christians who know enough to realize that they had better add—with all due reverence and a sense of community—"Our . . . who art in heaven."

So this is the first trait of grownup Christianity that Matthew wants to teach: a deep and communal reverence for God our Father—a reverence, I must say, sadly lacking at times on this very campus. For example, just a few moments ago we prayed, "Hallowed be thy name." Yet one is liable to walk out of this chapel and hear the name of God tossed around as irreverently as a bean-bag, usually in exclamations: "Oh my God!" "God, that was a hard exam!" Aren't you scared? Or don't you know enough to be scared? Grow up and get smart. Surely you aren't so young and wet behind the ears that you've never heard about the *final* final exam, the truly comprehensive one, and that Jesus said in Matthew 12:36–37, "Human beings will have to give an account of every careless word they've spoken. For by your words you'll be justified, and by your words you'll be condemned."

Going right along with reverence for God and God's name is respect for your fellow human beings, not only but especially for your fellow Christians. Matthew's church had grown large. It was probably located in a big city, because he inserts the word "city" no fewer than eighteen times where the other Gospels don't have it. With all the crowds joining the church, Christians were becoming suspicious of each other, as well they might. Preachers with charisma, but also with pecuniary motives, were gaining influence, popularity, and personal followings instead of followers of Jesus Christ. So church membership was mixed, false disciples with the true. Or to borrow from one of Jesus' parables, weeds were growing among the wheat. But—and here's the warning part of that parable—don't try to pull out the weeds. That's not your job, and it's not a job to be done now. Leave that to Jesus at the Last Day. "Judge not, lest you be judged." Your job is to take the plank out of your own eye so that you can restore your straying fellow Christians by taking the specks out of their eyes. Don't get angry with your fellow

Christians. Don't call them fools and blockheads. Don't question their claim to follow Jesus. Respect them for what they say they are. Jesus will judge their sincerity. Take care of your own.

Reverence for God translates into respect for others, and such respect shows itself in a variety of ways. It's a sign of maturity, for example, and especially of Christian maturity, not to have fun at others' expense, not to exhibit your cleverness by tearing them down, and not to laugh when someone else does the tearing down, or tells you about it, as though it were funny.

And if we respect one another—not just love one another—if we overcome our suspicions and respect each other, we'll also come to respect and love the one institution that binds us all together: the church. Many of you hardly know what the church is, because your Christianity comes from loose associations. They're very fine associations. I'm glad we have them, but in their very nature they're *loose* associations: Young Life clubs, Youth for Christ clubs, Christian youth camps, perhaps a church youth group (but often with lots more emphasis on youth than on church).

So you don't know the great hymns of the church. You don't know her forms and ceremonies and history. You don't know the history of your own denomination, if indeed you have a denomination. Maybe you don't even know what I mean by "denomination." I'm not blaming you if you don't. It's not your fault. But it's time you grow up, get interested, learn about the church, and participate in its life—not just in youth programs, but also in its wider, larger adult life.

That's part of Matthew's message, too. His is the only Gospel to mention the church: "I will build my church,"

Jesus says in Matthew 16:18, and "the gates of Hades will not prevail against it." The church is so institutional that Jesus compares it to a building. And in chapter 18 he says that the church—not individual Christians, but the church—should discipline its members. A church that disciplines can only be institutional. A pox on those who would prolong your adolescence by running down the institutionalism of the church in favor of loose Christian associations.

Sure, the church, like all institutions, can become big and bloated and impersonal and unexciting. It needs to go on a diet every once in a while, and liven up. It needs to thaw out and warm up. But it's the church of Jesus Christ: "I will build *my* church," he says. It's an institution without which you wouldn't be a Christian. It's the bulwark of the gospel. And in the end, you'll do a lot more good for the kingdom of God by giving your life to the church than by flitting from one fly-by-night parachurch ministry to another, from one exciting cross-cultural Christian experience to another.

Not that such ministries and experiences are bad. By no means! They can propel you into Christian service. They can enrich your Christian service. But just remember, in the long run the hard and sometimes boring work of the Christian church is what gets the job done, in this country and throughout the world. So don't go for excitement. Don't settle for the quick and easy. That's juvenile. Go for quality. Go for durability. Go for the institutional. Go for the church.

Now the church is a particular kind of institution, a religious one. To belong to it, then, you need to be a religious person. I know, I know: you've been told a hundred times if you've been told once—here, there, and everywhere—that Christianity isn't a religion, that it's a relationship, that Jesus undermined religion by befriending the irreligious people of his day (tax collectors and sinners), and that he attacked religion by criticizing the religious establishment of his day (scribes and Pharisees). Piffle! As we've already learned this morning, the same Jesus who seven times in Matthew 23 says, "Woe to you, scribes and Pharisees, hypocrites!" also says in Matthew 5:20, "Except your righteousness *exceeds* that of the scribes and Pharisees, you'll not enter the kingdom of heaven." That's *more* religion, not less.

How much more? Jesus spells it out in detail: It's not enough to avoid killing. Don't even get angry. It's not enough to avoid adultery. Don't even relish the imagination of it. It's not enough to give your wife a certificate of divorce so she can find another husband. Don't divorce her at all, and don't marry a divorcee. It's not enough to fulfill an oath. Don't even take one. It's not enough to practice justice toward others. Don't even strike back in the interests of justice for yourself. Love your enemies. Pray for your persecutors. Give charity, but don't be conspicuous about it. Pray, but don't be conspicuous about it. Fast, but don't be conspicuous about it. Be generous. Build up your account in heaven. Treat others the way you want them to treat you.

You can be sure that these commands were just as offensive to Jesus' original audience as they are to us. And he certainly didn't set such high standards just to make us feel so guilty and helpless that we'd cast ourselves on his mercy to forgive our failures, because the Gospel of Matthew reaches a climax with Jesus' parting words: "Go make disciples of all the nations . . . teaching them to obey absolutely everything that I've commanded you" (28:19–20). Now that's religion with a capital R.

But to obey absolutely everything Jesus commanded requires a knowledge of absolutely everything he commanded. No wonder, then, that he puts the Great Commission in the form of making disciples, because "disciples" means "learners, students": "Go make students of all the nations," students who learn Jesus' commandments. It's this learning that turns us into mature Christians, ones who can discriminate between good and bad, true and false, beautiful and ugly, tactful and deceitful, courteous and rude, refined and vulgar, excellent and tawdry, between the truly creative and the merely chaotic, between the admirable and the egotistical; learning that enables us to discriminate between love and sentiment, between liberty and license, between content and packaging, testifying and bragging, eloquence and claptrap, persuasion and manipulation, authentic wit and the buffoonery of jokes cheaply bought from among the penny stocks of predictably romantic, sexual, and scatological topics. Ho-hum.

The list could go on; but these and other distinctions become more and more important to us as we become adults, especially Christian adults, because ultimately—and often immediately—moral values attach to such distinctions. When we grow up, really grow up, crudity disgusts us rather than tickling us, because crudity demeans us all. Dignity, which differs from stuffiness, builds us up. When we grow up we enjoy serving more than being entertained. We're unimpressed by what's flashy, but deeply moved by what's profound, which used to make us yawn.

As you know, the Jews have developed a bar mitzvah ceremony. Sociologists would call it a rite of passage from being a minor in the Jewish religion to being an adult in that religion. The ceremony inducts Jewish young people into the privileges and responsibilities which adults have. "Bar mitzvah" means "son of the commandment"—in other words, somebody who has learned the commandments and is now expected to obey them. No more pleading of youthful ignorance. The whole of your Christian college education—the curriculum, the extra-curricular activities, the special lectures, the concerts, the dramatic productions, the art exhibits, the athletic competitions, the literary readings, the practicums—all are supposed to make you bar mitzvah. You're here to become daughters and sons of the commandments, Jesus' commandments. You're here to be inducted into Christian adulthood. So blow away the foam and start quaffing the thick brew of mature faith and practice. Discover pleasures you never dreamed existed.

The apostle Paul writes, "When the perfect comes, the partial will be put away. When I was a child, I spoke as a child, I thought as a child, I reasoned as a child. When I became a man, I put away childish things" (1 Corinthians 13:10–11). Paul is playing not only on the contrasts between a man and a child, and between the perfect and the partial. He's playing also on the parallels between the perfect and the man, and between the partial and the child. A man, an adult, is full grown, whole, mature, perfect. So Jesus says to his disciples, his students: "You shall be perfect/mature/adult, as your heavenly Father is perfect/ mature/adult." Otherwise God wouldn't be a father, would he?

Coming Home

~ Delivered at a Homecoming service in autumn ~

I suppose it makes sense for a scholar-*in-residence* like me to speak at *Home*coming, and *about* Homecoming. On the other hand, Homecoming—especially Homecoming Chapel—is a mix of contradictions. As students, the vast majority of you don't think of Westmont as your home. Even if you did, you're not *coming* home; you've already been here for a month. And you're looking forward to *going* home for the Fall Holiday in a couple of weeks. If you're homesick, you can hardly wait to go home to Mom and Dad, brothers, sisters, boyfriends, girlfriends.

But you alumni—you're a different kettle of fish. You were nurtured here as students. That's the very meaning of the word *alumni*. It comes from a Latin verb that means "to nurture." And *alma mater* means "a nurturing mother." You were nurtured here in many respects: socially, spiritually, and—not least, we hope—intellectually. So for you, Homecoming is *coming* home, not *going* home. It's coming home to Mother Westmont.

It's doubly a coming home for Kevin Vanhoozer (Alumnus of the Year) and for Judy Gundry. They not only attended Westmont; they grew up here. I don't know what to do with Nancy Favor Phinney, Karen Percival Gluck, Dana Alexander, and Cliff Lundberg. They not only attended Westmont and grew up here. They also live and work here right now. They're neither coming nor going.

So my first question: Why this difference on Homecoming between you current students, for whom the weekend isn't a Homecoming at all, and you alumni, for whom it's very much a Homecoming? Well, during college you're on perpetual probation. You feel under constant threat. You might flunk out, lose your scholarship, lose your athletic eligibility, be suspended, thrown out, or—perhaps worst of all—not earn good enough grades to get into the grad school of your choice. None of these possibilities carries the comforts of home!

The poet Robert Frost said famously, "Home is the place where, when you go there, they have to take you in." Now that you alumni are out of college, there's no more probation. There aren't any more threats. All is forgiven; we have to take you in. Even better than Frost's statement, we *rejoice* to take you in—just as in the parable of the prodigal son (though we don't suppose that in the "far country" you've been "wasting your substance in riotous living").

Here's another question that'll lead up to a passage of Scripture: What's the difference between a "home" and a "house"? Burchfield's *The New Fowler's Modern English Usage* notes that "estate agents . . . tend to work on the assumption that *home* is a more personal and warmer term than *house*." And sure enough, a look through the yellow pages of the phone book under "Real Estate" shows that most realtors don't say they sell houses. They say they sell homes, doubtless because "homes" has the flavor of "security . . . happiness . . . refuge . . . family" (*The American Heritage Dictionary*).

When you think of a house you think of a building, a structure made out of wood and stucco, bricks and mortar, cement, nails, shingles. When you think of a home you think of a house that's inhabited, that's lived in. You think of intimate personal relationships. You think of eating together at Thanksgiving, of opening presents around the Christmas tree, of conversing in front of a blazing fireplace. House is cold; home is cozy. You *buy* a house; you *live* in a home. Precisely because he didn't think of his father's house as a home, the elder brother didn't join the party at the homecoming of his prodigal brother.

A home is—well, we say, "homey." You'd never say "housey." You enter your front door and announce, "I'm home," not "I'm house." To get a loan you go to Home Savings and Loan, not House Savings and Loan. To buy materials for a repair job, you go down to the Home Improvement Center on Gutierrez Street, not the House Improvement Center. Of course, all this use of "home" where "house" would be more appropriate comes from advertising spin. But you get the point.

Now which word, "house" or "home," do you think really and truly fits better in Jesus' statement, "In my Father's house/home are many abodes" (John 14:2)? Notice that I said "abodes," not the "mansions" of the King James Version and lots of our gospel songs. "Mansions" gives the completely wrong notion of a fancy Montecito estate, like the one just up the road from where you turn into our main entrance. It's the same word you find in Jesus' statement in verse 23: "My Father will love the one who loves me and keeps my word, and we'll come to him and make our abode with him." The word is simply the noun corresponding to the verb "abide" in the next chapter of John's Gospel: "Abide in me, and I in you. As a vine can't bear fruit of itself unless it abides in the vineyard, so you can't bear fruit unless you abide in me" (15:4).

In view of these statements by Jesus, abiding carries two ideas. The first is an interpersonal relation so close it's like living inside the other person. Not just "like"—in a very real, spiritual sense it *is* living inside the other person. Second, abiding indicates an interpersonal relation so close it's permanent. An abode is a place where you stay, so that a number of modern translations use "remain" instead of "abide."

"Abide" and "abode" sound a bit old-fashioned, though. You don't go around saying you "abide" in your dorm room, do you? And I suspect you don't call your dorm room an "abode." But if you say "remain" in John 15 ("Remain in me, and I in you")—if you say "remain" instead of "abide," you lose the connection between "abodes" ("In my Father's house/home are many abodes") and "abide" ("Abide in me"). I haven't found a single English translation that shows the close connection between the "many abodes" in John 14:2 and "abiding" in Christ in the following chapter. What a shame! (I guess you'll just all have to take Greek.)

So back to my multiple choice question: In view of the intimate and permanent personal relation that abiding indicates, which word, "house" or "home," fits better with a place to abide? (a) "In my Father's *house* are many abodes" or (b) "In my Father's *home* are many abodes"? (a) or (b)? If you answered (a) you're wrong, and double off for the wrong answer, since you had a 50% chance of guessing right. "In my Father's *home* are many abodes."

Next question, a fill-in: What's the address of the Father's home? Where is it? What is it? You might think it's heaven, the New Jerusalem with pearly gates and streets of gold. But wait a minute. It so happens that the phrase "my Father's home" occurs earlier in John's Gospel—in chapter 2, to be exact. There, Jesus goes to Jerusalem at the Passover Festival of the Jews. In the temple he finds sellers of sacrificial animals and birds, and doesn't like what he sees. So he makes a whip out of some cords; drives out the merchants, their animals and birds; upsets the tables of the money-changers; and sends the coins flying to the floor. Then he says, "Take these things out of here. Stop making my Father's home a house of commerce."

You'll notice that I switched from "home" to "house": "Stop making my Father's *home* a *house* of commerce." It's actually the same word in the original text, but with a different nuance in its two occurrences. Jesus was objecting to the merchants' changing the temple, his Father's "home," into a mere "house," changing it from a place where God abides into a mere store building where buying and selling take place. Desecrated though it was, then, the Father's home looks to be the temple in Jerusalem.

But *is* it? There's more. When Jesus said to the merchants, "Stop making my Father's home a house of commerce," his disciples remembered that it's written in Psalm 69, "Zeal for your home will devour me/will consume me." Jesus' act of cleansing the temple was an act of zeal for God's home. And that act was going to devour him, consume him. You can't miss the ominous ring of these words. They sound a death knell for Jesus.

But there's *still* more. The Jews challenge Jesus' authority: "What sign do you show us, seeing that you're doing these things?" Jesus answered, "Dismantle this temple—destroy it, and in three days I'll raise it." The Jews ridicule Jesus' statement: "It took forty-six years to build this temple, and are you going to raise it in three days?" Then John explains: "But Jesus was talking about the temple of his body. So when he rose from the dead, his disciples remembered that he'd said this."

Is the temple in Jerusalem the Father's home, then? It was once upon a time. But not any more! It doesn't even exist any more. Jesus, his very body, the flesh that the Word who was with God and was God became—Jesus' very flesh is the Father's home, the true temple—because by definition a temple is where deity dwells; and God dwells, he abides, in the body of Jesus. No wonder Jesus says to the Samaritan woman at Jacob's well in John 4:21, "Believe me . . . the hour is coming . . . and now is . . . when you'll worship the Father neither on this mountain [Mount Gerizim, where the Samaritans worshiped] nor in Jerusalem." Jesus himself is now the place to worship God. No wonder he says to his disciples, "Abide in me." He himself is the place where God the Father abides. He himself is the Father's home. If you want a relation with God, then, you have to abide in Jesus, because he's the place where you'll find God, or where God will find you.

So "in my Father's home are many abodes" means "in me/in my body/in my flesh are many abodes." In his *body*? In his *flesh*? How can that be? Jesus continues in 14:2, "I'm going to prepare a place for you." Where is he going? To his Father in heaven? Ultimately, yes; but not yet. Jesus is speaking to his disciples in the Upper Room on the eve of his crucifixion. He's going to his Father in heaven later, but at the moment he's going to the cross. It's there, on the cross, at Golgotha, the Place of the Skull—as John calls it in chapter 19—it's there that Jesus prepared for us abiding places in his own body. There, at Golgotha, as Jesus' corpse hung on the cross, a soldier pierced his side, and out flowed blood and water. And for us who by faith drink his blood and eat his flesh, as he said we have to do if we want eternal life (John 6), the opening in his side that let out blood and water becomes our point of entry into his body, where we abide. It's a happy and secure place to be, just as a true home is. Our abodes aren't mansions in heaven, then. They're abiding places in Jesus' body, the home of God the Father.

A little over ten years ago, on January 14, 1993, our student newspaper, *The Horizon*, carried a story about Robert Earl Parsons. Robert lived in Hesperia here in California, but he'd come to Westmont as a transfer student. Two weeks away from his twenty-second birthday, during Christmas break—in fact, the morning after he'd returned from campus to Hesperia—Robert was killed in a car accident. His nineteen-year old sister Amy was in the car at the time, but survived. She said that the last thing she heard her brother say was, "I'm coming home, God." The accident happened directly in front of the residence of an elder at Grace Baptist Church, to which Robert and his family belonged.

The apostle Paul wrote, "We prefer to be absent from the body and at home with the Lord." So when we speak about a Christian's death, we speak about his or her *going* home to be with the Lord. But when Robert addressed God just before the collision that killed him, he talked about *coming* home. That was just right. As a Christian, Robert knew his correct address. He knew where his true home was, and is—where Jesus is. Since Jesus is the Word who was with God and was God, Robert could truthfully say, "I'm coming home, God."

But there's another way to understand "coming home," an even better way so far as our passage of Scripture is concerned. Jesus goes on to say, "If I go and prepare a place for you, *I'm* coming again, and I'll take you to myself that where I am you also may be."

We aren't the ones coming. *He*'s the one who's coming. He's the Father's home that's coming to take us to himself, so that by our abiding in him he can be *our* home as well as the *Father*'s home. "To myself," Jesus says. Of course, because in him, in his very flesh, are many abodes, a place for each of us who believe in him.

But do we have to wait for the so-called second coming to abide in him? No. Jesus refers to his second coming elsewhere, but not here. He came first into the world at his incarnation. He came again to his disciples right after his death and resurrection—in other words, right after his glorification. Listen to John 20:19: "Jesus *came* and stood in the midst of the disciples and said to them, 'Peace to you.'" According to 20:24, Thomas wasn't with them when Jesus "*came*" and stood in their midst. Eight days later, according to 20:26, Jesus "*comes*" and stands in the midst of them (including Thomas this time). According to 21:13, Jesus "*comes*" to his disciples at the lakeside in Galilee.

John is the only New Testament writer to use the verb "come" for the recently risen Jesus. All the other writers talk only about Jesus' *appearing* to the disciples and about their *seeing* him. So when in John 14 Jesus tells his disciples just before the crucifixion that he's coming again, he's referring to what from our standpoint has already happened. He came again to the disciples right after his glorification.

Ah, but there *is* a still future coming of Jesus in John's Gospel. Chapter 21, verses 22–23, record that after he'd come again several times the risen Jesus said, "If I want the beloved disciple to abide [that is, stay alive] *till I come*, what is that to you, Peter? Follow me." Jesus didn't say the beloved disciple wasn't going to die, only "*if* I want him to stay alive till I come." So Jesus' comings right after his glorification to take us into our abodes in his own body, pierced at the crucifixion—those comings anticipated his coming yet in our future.

In the book of Revelation, then, John writes about Jesus, "Behold, he's *coming* with clouds, and every eye will see him, even those who pierced him" (1:7). And he quotes Jesus: "Yes, I'm *coming* quickly" (Revelation 22:20a). So again, "coming home" doesn't mean that we're coming home. It means that Jesus, the Father's home who has now become our home too, is coming, just as he came to the disciples right after his glorification. The Christian response is, "Amen! *Come*, Lord Jesus," to which is added a benediction, "The grace of the Lord Jesus be with all who hear the words of the prophecy of this book" (Revelation 22:20b–21).

That benediction ends the Book of Revelation. But I want to add a footnote. (After all, a would-be scholar without a footnote is like the emperor without his clothes.) Here's the footnote: In Revelation 3:12 John quotes Jesus as saying, "I'll make the one who wins the victory [in other words, who proves to be a true Christian]—I'll make the one who wins the victory a pillar in the temple of my God." You've doubtless seen photos of ancient Greek and Roman pillars sculpted in the shape of human beings, like the caryatids (female figures) in the porch of the Erechtheum on the Acropolis in Athens. Remember now that according to John 2, Jesus is the new and true temple of God, God's home. To be made a pillar in God's temple, then, is to abide in Jesus not only now, but also forever. For the promise in Revelation 3:12 goes on to say that those who, by winning the victory, become pillars in God's temple, Jesus, will never go out of that temple. Naturally they won't. Pillars don't walk! In him there's security for all eternity.

And then Jesus promises that he'll inscribe on these victorious pillars the name of God, the name of the New

Jerusalem, and his own new name. Later the book of Revelation says the New Jerusalem doesn't have a temple, because the Lord God Almighty and the Lamb Jesus are its temple (21:22). And what is the New Jerusalem? Not the place where we Christians will dwell forever. *What* is the New Jerusalem? is the wrong question. *Who* is the New Jerusalem? John's answer is, "the bride, the wife of the Lamb" (21:9). The New Jerusalem is we Christian victors, the bride and wife of Jesus the Lamb, but portrayed as a shining city in which there's no temple except for God and Jesus. Notice: *in* which there's no temple except for God and Jesus. God and Jesus are the temple in the New Jerusalem, and we are that city. So God and Jesus abide in us just as we abide in them. We're their home just as they're our home—forever and ever. May this Homecoming remind us, then, of our home who has already come, and will yet come.

Traditional Nonliturgical Worship

~ Delivered for a chapel series on worship ~

Welcome to Worship 101. This is the first in a series of three chapels representing three traditions of Christian worship, three different styles of worship. But the differences aren't limited to style. They have to do with substance, too. The purpose isn't to make value judgments. You can do that for yourselves. The purpose is to draw distinctions and explain them. Of course, many churches have hybrid forms of worship, combinations of different styles and substance; but we're talking about more or less pure forms. Later there'll be a chapel representing contemporary worship with guitars, maybe an electric keyboard, drums, praise songs, hand-raising, clapping, maybe even some dancing in the aisles—anyway, a lot of spontaneous audience participation, the kind of service you'd find especially in a charismatic church or a church where people feel free to come wearing a tank top and jeans and sipping a cup of coffee. A liturgical chapel will represent just the opposite: readings of set prayers and confessions and thanksgivings, the recitation of an ancient creed, kneeling, incense, bells, fancy vestments for the clergy, and above all a celebration of the Lord's Supper, the Eucharist, complete with lots of symbolic gestures—everything prescribed and orderly, the kind of service you'd find in a Roman Catholic or Episcopalian church.

Today's chapel represents the kind of service you'd find in a Baptist or Presbyterian church that hasn't converted to the contemporary style. It's more formal than the contemporary, but less formal than the liturgical. We have here a piano instead of a pipe organ or a guitar. We'll sing hymns instead of praise songs. I'm not wearing jeans; but I'm not wearing vestments, either. If I were a Presbyterian I'd be wearing a robe, but that's a little too formal for a

Baptist like me. I'm not slaying people in the Spirit, so that they fall on the floor; and I'm not a priest representing people to God or offering a eucharistic sacrifice to God. I'm a preacher.

What's important about this kind of service is the Word of God. The contemporary or charismatic service emphasizes what we say to each other in the Spirit, using our spiritual gifts to help each other worship. The liturgical service emphasizes what we say to God through a priest. This service emphasizes what God says to us through his Word. So a church of this kind that's completely true to its tradition doesn't have to put Bibles in the pews. People bring their own Bibles, and they sit out in front of the preacher in direct earshot, not in a semicircle as though it were a sharing session. The pulpit stands on an elevated platform with an oversized Bible resting on it; and the pulpit is in the middle of the platform, not pushed off to one side by the communion table or an altar. The communion table is demoted to floor level and used only once a month. The pulpit emphasizes God's Word. It's massive and heavy, not some flimsy lectern you could push over by leaning on it.

In a contemporary service, especially a charismatic one, the congregation does most of the work. In a liturgical service the priest does the heavy lifting. In a service of the Word, the preacher does it. But because of the big pulpit, you can hardly see him. It's the Word of God that's central and weighty. Ultimately, the preacher doesn't count. He's just a talking head, a microphone for God's Word. That's the reason I haven't introduced myself to those of you who don't know me. The Word of God—that's what counts. So everything builds up to the sermon. It, not the Eucharist or an after-meeting of prayer and praise and testimony and healing—the sermon is the climax; and it's long, a half-hour or more, not the fifteen-minute homily (Baptists would dismiss it as a sermonette) you get in the middle of a liturgical service. I've heard sermons that were nearly two hours long (and held your attention, I might add). You don't clap. You don't applaud. You listen. You repent. You believe. You obey. The Lord is speaking through the preached Word. Let all the earth keep silence before him.

The Scripture reading is geared to the sermon, not to the Christian calendar with all its holy days and holy weeks. Even the hymns and special music lead up to the sermon, and the closing hymn responds to the preached Word. The hymns aren't like praise songs that have a few words sung in unison over and over again to set a worshipful mood. The hymns are like the sermon; they have many words to convey the message of God's Word as fully as possible. The music is crisp. It doesn't blur. It doesn't slip and slide from one note to another, because it's supposed to help send a clear message more than setting a mood. (Not that mood-setting is wrong; I'm just pointing out a difference from praise songs.) Since the hymns are long and wordy, three or four stanzas or more, what you lose in emotional effect you gain in theological content. Four-part harmony suits this greater complexity; so you have the music printed in front of you instead of having the words flashed on a screen without any musical notations. You have the music printed in front of you, and you sing in harmony. Instead of a worship team you have a single song leader who beats the time to keep the tempo from lagging under the weight of all this content. Let's start our service of the Word, then.

There followed a hymn, a sermon (for an expanded version of which see the next talk), another hymn, and a benediction.

God Loved the World in Aramaic, Latin, and Greek: John 3:16 according to John 19:19-20

~ Delivered as a keynote address at an on-campus conference of foreign language teachers ~

To address the topic, "God Loved the World in Aramaic, Latin, and Greek," I'd like to juxtapose two texts in the Gospel of John and treat them in terms of the larger context of John's writings as distinct from the rest of the New Testament, especially from the other Gospels. Let's take the texts in reverse order. First, John 19:19–20: "And Pilate . . . wrote a title and put in on the cross, and it was written, 'Jesus the Nazarene, the King of the Jews.' . . . and it was written in Aramaic, Latin, Greek." Why these three languages? Well, Aramaic was a Semitic language closely related to Hebrew as, say, Dutch to German. In fact, Aramaic came so close to Hebrew that the Greek New Testament, including this very text, probably uses the word "Hebrew" to mean "Aramaic," as we can tell from other texts where "Hebrew" describes words that have an Aramaic spelling which differs slightly from the Hebrew spelling. The most famous example of such a difference is *abba*, Aramaic for "father," as compared with the Hebrew *ab*, without the final *ba*, as in the first part of the name "Absalom," which means "father of [or 'is'] peace," *ab-shalôm*.

There's Aramaic. As to Latin, it was the language of the Roman government, of course. So its mention reminds us of the Roman as well as Jewish framework of Jesus' crucifixion. John puts it this way in 19:16 of his Gospel: "Then . . . he [the Roman governor, Pontius Pilate] delivered him [Jesus] to them [the Jewish chief priests] in order that he might be crucified." But despite its official status, Latin hadn't caught hold throughout the Roman Empire. Most nearly universal of all was the Greek language because of Alexander the Great's conquests and the ensuing hellenization of conquered territories. And later, though the Romans conquered the Greeks militarily, the Greeks conquered the Romans culturally, as shown by the writing of the New Testament entirely in Greek. Think of it: the apostle Paul wrote to the Roman Christians in Greek, not in Latin. So the inscription on Jesus' cross "was written in Aramaic, Latin, Greek," that is, in ever-widening circles of linguistic use.

Now turn your attention with me to the most beloved text in the New Testament: John 3:16. You know it by heart, I'm sure; so I hope you don't think it's beneath your scholarly dignity to consider such a familiar verse of Scripture. I know there's something to be said for not spoiling certain verses of Scripture with commentary or interpretation. They shine with a purity so pristine that it seems a shame to do more than quote them. If such verses exist, John 3:16 is surely among them. But I'll take the risk of spoilage in the hope of enrichment. "For God so loved the world that he gave the only Son, that everyone believing in him might not perish, but have eternal life."

There are several mistakes to make about the meaning of this Golden Text of Christianity. Or so it seems to me. The first is to do what I just did, quote the verse in isolation. By traditional rules of grammar, John 3:16 isn't even a complete sentence—just four clauses in a sentence that starts with verse 14 and carries right through verse 17. And the clauses that make up verse 16 are only dependent ones at that. You'll find the sole independent clause in the second half of verse 14: "thus it is necessary that the Son of Man be lifted up." Everything else is dependent, subordinate, from the start of verse 14 through the end of verse 17.

"And just as Moses lifted up the serpent in the wilderness" provides an analogy for the necessity of the Son of Man's being lifted up—a divine necessity. "That everyone believing may have eternal life in him" tells the purpose of that necessity. "For God so loved the world" gives an explanation, or reason, for the lifting up of the Son of Man. "That he gave the only Son" exhibits the result of God's having loved the world." ("*The* only Son" means "*his* only Son," for the Greek definite article can function as a weak possessive.) Giving the Son had, in turn, a negative purpose, "that everyone believing in him might not perish," plus a positive purpose, "that [everyone believing in him] might have eternal life." Just as the necessity of the Son of Man's being lifted up had an explanation in God's loving the world, so now God's loving the world has its own explanation in God's sending the Son into the world. One possible purpose for that sending is denied: "for God did not send the Son into the world in order that he might judge the world." Another purpose is affirmed: "but [God did send his Son into the world] in order that the world might be saved through him." End of sentence—finally.

Or should we start a new sentence with the first "that" in verse 16? "For God so loved the world *that* . . . ." The Greek word underlying "that" is really made up of two words meaning "and so" (a completely different "so," by the way, from the "so" in "God so loved the world"), and this double-sided word can easily introduce a main clause. If we should start a new sentence here in the middle of verse 16, "For God so loved the world" ends the sentence begun in verse 14. "And so God gave his only Son" then starts a new sentence with a statement that parallels and interprets the earlier statement about the necessity of the Son of Man's being lifted up; and the purpose clause in verse 16, "in order that everyone believing . . ." likewise parallels the purpose-clause in verse 15, which also begins, "in order that everyone believing . . . ."

Whether or not we start a new sentence in the middle of John 3:16, the first mistake is to isolate this verse from its context. The second is to misunderstand the combination "so . . . that": "For God *so* loved the world that he gave his only Son." I'd take odds that most people understand that statement to mean, "For God loved the world so *much* that he gave his only Son." Why, that's the very translation you'll find in some English versions. You'll find the same mistake in many commentaries. I call it a mistake because "so" means "thus, in this way." "And so" indicates the *result* of the way God loved the world, not the *degree* of his love. "Just as Moses lifted up the serpent in the wilderness, so/in this way it is necessary that the Son of Man be lifted up," *not* "to this degree it is necessary that the Son of Man be lifted up." And elsewhere throughout the Gospel and Epistles of John and his book of Revelation, this "so" indicates manner, not amount.

The third mistake is to think that this "so" points forward to God's giving the Son: "For God so loved the world that he gave his only Son." But everywhere else in John, and in 1–3 John and Revelation too (with one possible exception, and I'm not sure even of it), "so" points backward to something earlier. Take this very passage, for example: "And just as Moses lifted up the serpent in the wilderness, so/in this way it is necessary that the Son of Man be lifted up." The manner of the Son of Man's being lifted up harks back to Moses' lifting up the serpent. And the manner of

God's loving the world harks back, in turn, to the Son of Man's being lifted up.

What then is this lifting up that defines God's loving the world? It's still future in John 8:28, where Jesus says to his enemies, "Whenever you lift up the Son of Man . . . ." But the reference becomes editorially clear in 12:32–34: "And I, if I be lifted up from the earth, will draw all to myself," Jesus states. Then John adds, "And this he said signifying by what sort of death he was going to die. The crowd therefore answered him, 'We have heard from the Law that the Christ abides forever, and how is it that you say, "It is necessary that the Son of Man be lifted up?"'" (You'll notice that Jesus hasn't said anything about divine necessity on *this* occasion; so the text in chapter 12 must be echoing the divine necessity of the Son of Man's being lifted up all the way back in chapter 3, where Jesus conversed with Nicodemus.)

Now earlier in his Gospel—that is, earlier than chapter 12—John made a big point of the Jews' failure on two occasions to stone Jesus: "'Before Abraham was, I am.' Therefore they picked up stones to throw at him. But Jesus hid himself and went out of the temple" (8:58–59); "'I and my Father are one.' Again the Jews picked up stones to stone him . . . . and he escaped from their hand" (10:30–31, 39). And later in the Gospel, "The Jews said to Pilate, 'We're not permitted to execute anyone.' [They said this] in order that Jesus' word might be fulfilled, what he had said signifying by what sort of death he was going to die" (18:31–32).

What's a stoning, then? It's a knocking down, rather like the stumbling that Jesus mentions in reply to the disciples when they try to persuade him against reentering Judea lest he be stoned: "Rabbi, the Jews are now seeking to stone you, and are you going there again?" (11:8). But there are "twelve hours in a day" (11:9), and Jesus' "hour" hasn't yet come (8:20). So he won't stumble against a stone and fall down any more than the Jews can knock him down with stones. His death will direct him upward, not downward. It'll be a crucifixion, not a stoning, a lifting up, not a knocking down. Exaltation doesn't wait for ascension, as throughout the rest of the New Testament. Not in John! Here exaltation *is* crucifixion. Crucifixion turns *into* exaltation, *becomes* exaltation.

Gone, then, is all shame from Jesus' crucifixion in John. Gone is the insulting kiss by Judas, the disciples' faithless flight, the degrading seizure of Jesus. The Jesus of John presents himself voluntarily—and on his own terms by insisting that the disciples be let go (18:1–9): "Whom do you seek?" "Jesus the Nazarene." "I'm [he]." Again, "Whom do you seek?" "Jesus the Nazarene." "I told you I'm [he]. So if you seek me, let these go away." No longer does Simon Peter curse Jesus, as we should probably understand Mark 14:71. Jesus talks back to his Jewish judge, and converses with Pilate, and once even interrogates Pilate (18:33–19:11). No sheep silent before its shearers here. Not as elsewhere, Jesus *did* open his mouth. You don't expect the Logos, the Word, to keep quiet, do you? Even the scurrilous accusations against Jesus disappear from John. Replacing them are the true statements that Jesus made himself out to be the Son of God, and a king. Gone is the spitting on Jesus, his being blindfolded, fisticuffed, taunted to prophesy, beaten on the head with a reed. The scourging and slapping do stay in John's account, also the crowning with thorns and clothing with purple. But even there the vocabulary of mockery is gone, as is the later ridicule of Jesus while he hangs on the cross.

John bends the whole episode toward the declaration of Pilate that despite the third degree, he finds Jesus innocent, and above all toward the contrast between Pilate's declaration, "Behold, the human being! [*Ecce homo*!]" and Jesus' self-identification as the Son of God. Matthew and Mark tell us that the soldiers who had put the royal purple on Jesus took it off before leading him to Golgotha. Not in John: He "came out wearing the crown of thorns and the purple robe" (19:5). True, at the scene of crucifixion the soldiers take Jesus' own clothing for themselves. But for all we can tell he continues to wear the purple robe, as well as the crown, on the cross, as on a throne.

In Mark and Matthew, the inscription that's placed on the cross makes up an accusation against Jesus, the legal charge under which he was executed, in immediate conjunction with the execution of two bandits. In Luke, the inscription forms part of the mockery of Jesus, in immediate conjunction with the high priests' and soldiers' ridiculing him. But in John the inscription honors Jesus as the King of the Jews. Otherwise the Jews wouldn't have asked Pilate to reword it to the effect that Jesus *said*, "I am King of the Jews" (19:21); and Pilate's refusal to change the wording preserves this honor paid to Jesus.

The seamless tunic is singled out as undivided, untorn. There's no ridicule from the bandits crucified with Jesus, not even from the unrepentant one. No darkness descends. It can't eclipse this sun/Son. As already in John's prologue, darkness doesn't overcome the light of life (1:5). The light of the world is shining from this lampstand of a cross (8:12). Gone is the Cry of Dereliction, "My God, my God, why hast thou forsaken me?" (How can the Word who *is* God be forsaken *by* God?) Instead, Jesus calmly takes care of his personal affairs ("Woman, behold your son," he says to his mother concerning the beloved disciple, and vice versa to him), just as he calmly prayed for his disciples throughout the whole of chapter 17 rather than throwing himself on the ground in a sweat of emotional turmoil and praying about his own fate as in Mark, Matthew, and Luke.)

Jesus takes wine at his own initiative ("I thirst"). He proclaims his signs, works, and words finished, bows his head, and with all deliberation gives over the Spirit, as John puts it in 19:30. Jesus is spared the leg-breaking. The side-piercing releases the atoning blood and the water of the Spirit, to make available his blood for drinking (chapter 6) and to fulfill the promise in 7:37–39 concerning "rivers of living water": "He spoke this concerning the Spirit, which people believing in him were about to receive. For the Spirit wasn't yet [given], because Jesus wasn't yet glorified." But by his crucifixion he *has* been glorified, so that the Spirit gushes in torrents from his pierced side. (In the Middle East, "rivers" [plural] means torrents of water such as swell the usually dry creek beds after a heavy downpour.) Jesus' body doesn't get a merely proper burial. It gets a sumptuous one: in a garden, in a new tomb where no corpse has yet been laid, and with a hundred pounds of spices. No shame here. No dishonor. No humiliation. Instead, honor and glory.

No wonder the Johannine Jesus says on the eve of his crucifixion, "Now is the Son of Man glorified" (13:31). What a *tour de force*! According to the apostle Paul, "the word of the cross is . . . a scandal to the Jews and folly to Gentiles"; according to Justin Martyr in the second century, "madness." With crude mockery an ancient Roman graffito portrays Jesus as having the head of an ass as he hangs on the cross. So John's making the cross of

Jesus into his glorification is like making the gas chamber at Buchenwald into the Sistine Chapel. But he did it! John did it! The cross of Jesus lifts him up to glory, so that he draws all to himself (12:32). Ordinarily the sight of crucifixion repulses people. But not *Jesus*' crucifixion. So there they are, representatives of those "all" whom he draws: his mother and her sister, the wife of Clopas and Mary Magdalene, plus the beloved disciple—not standing at a distance, as in the Synoptic Gospels, but at the very foot of the cross, close enough for private conversation with Jesus. The uplifted magnet of salvation has drawn them to himself: "you who used to be far off have been made near by the blood of Christ" (to borrow Paul's statement in Ephesians 2:13). The King of the Jews, represented by Aramaic, has become the loadstone of salvation for Romans and Greeks, too, speakers of Roman (that's the underlying word for Latin in John's text) and speakers of Greek. High on the cross, he fulfills the wish of those Greeks in chapter 12 who at the triumphal entry, after the Pharisees had said to each other in dismay, "Look! The world has gone after him!" came to Philip (you'll note his Greek name) and said, "Sir, we want to see Jesus." Well, you Greeks and all others who've come from afar to celebrate the Passover, you can see him now, the true Passover, high and lifted up, like the Lord of hosts in Isaiah's inaugural vision.

That's the way God loved the world, by making Jesus' crucifixion exalt him, elevate him to glory—not in one *fell* swoop, but in one *up*ward sweep—so that he might draw the all of the world to himself through giving them the water of the Spirit of life that flows from his pierced side, along with his blood that takes away the sin of the world in accordance with John the Baptist's proclamation at 1:29 of this Gospel. "God so loved the world" doesn't tell the

Christmas story, then. It tells the story of Passion Week. Not the story of birth (the nativity is missing from John), not even of incarnation (though John does have that), but the story of death by exaltation, of exaltation by death. The setting isn't the manger in Bethlehem, but the garden of Golgotha.

What kind of a world is it that God so loved there and then? Not the world that God pronounced good at the dawn of creation, not "my Father's world" in which "all nature sings and round me rings the music of the spheres" so that "I rest me in the thought of rocks and trees, of skies and seas." Not that world, romanticized so much nowadays in popular Christian devotional literature, complete with scenic, softlight photographs, as an antidote to urban malaise. No, God loved another kind of world, a world laden with sin (chapter 1), filled with lusts, inflated with pride (1 John 2:15–17); a world that didn't recognize the divine Word who entered it even though it came into being through him (John's Prologue again); a world that hasn't known God the Father, either; a world shrouded in darkness and bedeviled by false prophets and antichrists, situated in the Evil One (1 John), ruled by Satan, the father of lies, and therefore unable to receive the Spirit of truth; a world that hates and persecutes Jesus and his disciples, out of which he has chosen them, to which neither he nor they belong (John 17); a world that rejoices over his death; a world under judgment, that with its lusts is passing away, that his disciples aren't to love. In John, "Love one another [in the Christian community]" replaces "love your neighbor as yourself [whoever that neighbor is]." "Love one another," but "do *not* love the world." It's a world that Jesus explicitly says he doesn't even pray for ("I do not pray for the world" [John 17:9]). Imagine! A world that lies outside the purview of Jesus' praying! This worst of all possible worlds, this is the world that God loved.

Who is this God that loved such a world? The God who is light, in whom there is no darkness at all (1 John 1:5). The God of light loved the world of darkness. We'll never plumb the depths of "God so loved the world" without understanding the kind of world God loved, and the kind of God who loved such a world. Since John shows signs of Paul, and since according to Paul's most astonishing statement—the most astonishing in the whole Bible, I think—that whereas one transgression (the original sin) triggered condemnation, the many transgressions that followed, far from increasing condemnation, triggered justification (Romans 5:16), I'm tempted to say, that *because of* the world's sin, not despite it, God loved the world.

John 3:16—the only place in the entirety of Johannine literature where God directs his love to the world. And the result of this love? "He gave his only Son." We're back to Calvary. This isn't a Christmas gift; it's a gift of Passiontide. The uplifting of the Son of Man on the cross results in the giving of the Son of God for the life of the world. The benefit to the Son of Man Jesus—the turning of his crucifixion into his exaltation—translates into a gift for the world.

> Moses didn't give you the bread from heaven; rather, my Father gave you bread from heaven, the true bread . . . . I am the living bread that came down from heaven. If anyone eats of this bread, he will live forever; and the bread that I will give is my flesh, for the life of the world . . . . unless you eat the flesh of the Son of Man, and drink his blood, you don't have life in yourselves. The

> person who does eat my flesh and drink my blood
> has eternal life (John 6:32–33, 51, 53–54).

The Word *became* flesh that he might *give* his flesh, sacrificially separated from his blood; and that gift defines God's giving his only Son out of love for the world.

In other religions, human beings give sacrifice to the gods, not so much to satisfy the gods' righteous indignation at human wickedness. The gods themselves aren't righteous. Just read the myths about them; they read like soap operas. The gods themselves aren't righteous, much less loving. So offer them sacrifices to curry their favor, or at least to keep them from meddling in your life. Who ever heard of a god providing in love a sacrifice for human beings? John 3:16 turns the world of comparative religion upside down. But here it is—the astounding topsy-turvy! Where human beings ought to have been giving to God, he gave to human beings. Just as in Genesis 22, God himself provides a lamb for sacrifice, the lamb of God who takes away the world's sin. Only here, God provides himself as a sacrifice; for the given Son is none other than the Word who was in the beginning with God and *was* God, the only God who, being in the bosom of the Father, has given the world a divine exegesis of divine love in a divine gift. For the only God of 1:18 (the best and earliest manuscripts read "God," not "Son")—the only God of 1:18 is the only Son of 3:16.

The *only* Son of God. "O Absalom, my son, my son," David lamented at the loss of Absalom (2 Samuel 19:5). But David had other sons. One of them (Solomon) succeeded him on Israel's throne. Like it or not, we know the importance of sons in ancient society because of inheritance and carrying on the family line. What makes John 3:16 especially striking is that elsewhere John emphasizes in the strongest possible terms the Father's love for the Son. "The Father loves the Son and has given all things into his hand" (3:35). "The Father loves the Son and shows him all things that he himself is doing" (5:20), as though the Son were an apprentice, lovingly taught by the father his trade.

In fact, the love of God for his Son is the standard by which other loves are measured: "According as the Father loved me, I also have loved you." Jesus says to his disciples (15:9); and to his Father he says, "You have loved them according as you have loved me" (17:23). God's love for the world doesn't set the standard, then. His love for the Son does. The standard is Christocentric, not anthropocentric. That's what makes so striking God's giving his only Son in consequence of loving the world, this stinking, rotting world of sinful society—already four days' dead, like Lazarus's corpse (11:39). To this world God in love gave his only Son, the very Son on whom his love is supremely set.

Now we come to the end of the matter. I mean "end" not in the sense of bringing this address to a close, but in the sense of purpose and—happily—an end that has no end: "that every one believing in him [the Son] might not perish, but have eternal life." Time fails to spin out all the nuances—but just sketchily, "everyone" both individualizes the collective category of "the world" as human society and insures that nobody in that category needs to feel left out. Divine election there is, and it makes a strong appearance elsewhere in John; but it's not an election that should cause fear of omission. Election should comfort believers, not frighten unbelievers. Unbelievers have quite enough to fear without having to contend with the doctrine of election. "Everyone" holds out a promise, not a threat.

"Believing in [the Son]"—you know, I'm sure, the dynamic quality of believing—always a verb in John's Gospel, never a noun. So dynamic in fact, that believing counts as a work: "'Don't work for the food that perishes but for the food that abides to life eternal . . . .' 'What should we do that we may work the works of God [that is, do the works that he requires us to do]?' Jesus answered and said to them, 'This is the work of God [not the work that God does, which wouldn't fit Jesus' commanding his audience to work for the food that abides]—this is the work of God [the work that God requires], that you believe in him whom that one sent'" (John 6:27–29).

You never catch Paul making a statement like that. For him, belief and works belong to different categories: "To the person who works the reward isn't reckoned according to grace, but according to debt. But to the person who doesn't work but believes on the one who treats the ungodly person as righteous, his belief is reckoned as righteousness" (Romans 4:4–5); ". . . through belief . . . . not of works, lest anyone boast" (Ephesians 2:8–9). Even James maintains the distinction: Works show belief; apart from works, belief is dead, useless. Belief works together with works (with that statement James comes close to John), and belief is completed by works. But in John, belief *is* a work, is *the* work that God requires—active, dynamic, persevering, durative (most instances of the verb being in a tense that points to duration). And not just believing Jesus as a matter of intellectual assent, as in 4:21 and 14:11 ("Believe me, woman"; and to the disciples: "Believe me"). Believing in Jesus—a matter of personal commitment. To believe *Jesus* is to trust that he's telling you the truth. To believe *in* Jesus goes further: it's to entrust your fate into his hand, the hand out of which no one can snatch you.

This believing in Jesus grows out of believing *that*—specifically, that he is in the Father and the Father in him, as he said at the Last Supper (14:10–11), so that entrusting your fate into his hand is entrusting your fate into his Father's hand, out of which (again) no one can snatch you (10:27–30). It's believing that he's the Holy One of God, as Peter confessed him to be (6:69), so that entrusting your fate into his hand keeps you from the Devil, the Evil One. It's believing that he is I AM (8:58), so that entrusting your fate into his hand brings you into his eternity. Believing that he's the Christ, the Anointed One, so that his anointing you with the Spirit teaches you about all things true (1 John 2:27). Believing that he's the Son of God, so that entrusting your fate to him makes you a child of God. Believing that he came from God (16:30), believing that God sent him (11:42), so that entrusting your fate into his hand means washing in the Pool of Siloam, translated "Sent," cleansed and born from above by the water of the Spirit (chapter 9).

"Should not perish, should not be lost, destroyed"—the verb occurs elsewhere in John for perishable food (6:12). It's used for killing (10:10) and dying (11:50; 12:25). Here it stands in opposition to having eternal life. So it refers to what John in the book of Revelation calls "the second death," which he describes as being thrown into the lake of fire, a lake of liquid lava still red-hot and molten, not yet cooled and hardened. Do you feel uncomfortable with this language, as I do? Do you wish I'd take up the question of literal versus figurative interpretation and turn these expressions into a hermeneutical exercise? Sorry, but I'm not going to. To perish is to suffer the second death, to be thrown into the lake of fire. Whatever that entails, if the first thing we think about when hearing such language is how we can soften it, temper it, tame it, finesse it with a C. S. Lewis-*Great Divorce*-kind-of job, then—well, we've gotten too educated and cultured. Our first thought should be one of horror, utter horror.

Our second thought should be one of wild relief at not perishing if we've believed in Jesus. Let the hermeneutical question wait till our feelings of horror and relief have really gripped us. But there's another definition of perishing that needs mention. It too comes from the book of Revelation: "Outside are the dogs and the sorcerers and the fornicators and the murderers and the idolaters and everyone who loves and practices lying" (22:15). To perish is to be outside—outside the Celestial City, the New Jerusalem, outside the safety of its walls, outside its gates, forever unable to enter its gates of pearl even though they're never shut, outside the tabernacle of God, outside the temple which *is* God and the Lamb, outside its lamplight, the very glory of God, outside—perished, lost, lost in space, sucked into the black hole of outer darkness, from whose vortex there's no escape, not even a hope of escape ("Abandon hope, all ye who enter here"), the ultimate alienation, the dreadful reverse of having an abode in the Father's house, the woeful mother of all tears, sorrow, crying, pain, and death. "Should *not* perish," though, "but have eternal life." What boundless good news! "Life"—the very life of God and Christ, because to know them is to have this life (17:3). "Eternal life"—not just everlasting life, but life having the very quality of eternity, the age to come, when God has wiped away every tear from the eyes of the saved, has banished their sorrow, quieted their crying, relieved their pain, delivered them from death, and for them made all things new—life of unimprovable quality.

But I'd like to defend the King James Version, too: "everlasting life," "life without end" (to borrow from the Dead Sea Scrolls [1QS 4:7; CD 3:20]). Some stress needs to fall on perpetuity—"everlasting." "Don't work for the food that is perishing, but for the food that *abides* unto life eternal" (6:27). Elsewhere too, in other connections, eternity is associated with abiding, staying, remaining. "We've heard out of the Law that the Christ abides forever/eternally/everlastingly" (12:34). "The slave doesn't abide in the house forever/eternally/everlastingly" (8:35). "If what you heard from the beginning abides in you, you also will abide in the Son and in the Father; and this is the promise that he himself promised us: everlasting life" (1 John 2:24–25). "The one who does God's will abides forever/eternally/everlastingly"—doesn't "pass away" (1 John 2:17).

Oh the brevity of life! We spend our years as a tale that is told, and it's a *short* story. How quickly the grass withers, the flower fades, the candle flickers out. But "the one who eats this bread will live forever" (6:58). "Everyone who lives and believes in me will never die—forever" (11:26). Life eternal and everlasting, not because time*less* (with apologies to St. Augustine), but because time*ful*, so full of time that it's life without remainder, not because nothing remains, but because all remains. A bank account of life that grows with each expenditure. "I have come that they might have life," Jesus said, "and that they might have it abundantly" (*perisson* in Greek, "more than enough"—quantity in excess of need).

To have this life is to have Jesus Christ, for "eternal life" is also a christological title: "And the life was manifested, and we have seen him, and are bearing witness to him, and announcing to you the Eternal Life which was with the Father [for the Eternal Life is none other than the Word who was in the beginning with the Father]" (1 John 1:2); "This one [the Father's Son, Jesus Christ] is the true God and Eternal Life ([capital E, capital L]." To receive the gift of God's only Son is to have eternal life, for the Son *is* eternal life.

Back to the inscription, then: "'Jesus the Nazarene, the King of the Jews' . . . written in Aramaic, Latin, Greek." There's another king in Johannine literature. We read about him in that horrifying apocalyptic vision of the demonic locusts who swarm out of the bottomless pit, the abyss of hell: "And they have over them a king, the angel of the abyss. In Aramaic his name is Abaddon, and in Greek he has the name Apollyon" (Revelation 9:11). "Abaddon" means "destruction." "Apollyon" means "destroyer," a noun form of the verb "perish, be destroyed" in John 3:16. But it's also a derogatory pun on the name of the Greek god Apollo, with whom some of the Roman emperors identified themselves, and one of whose symbols was the locust. Aramaic and Greek—Latin is missing so as not to disturb the assonance of "Abaddon" and "Apollyon" or divert attention from the pun on Apollo, in whose name the allusion to Roman emperors makes up for the omission of Latin, anyway.

So here we have a parody of the inscription on Jesus' cross. Satan, a king from below. Jesus, the king from above. Satan, a king who destroys. Jesus, the king who builds: "Destroy this temple and in three days I will raise it"—a rebuilding of his body in resurrection, which he himself performs as the builder (John 2:19–22). Not as elsewhere in the New Testament, where Jesus is raised (passive voice). No, in John Jesus raises himself: "No one takes my life from me, but I lay it down of my own accord. I have authority to lay it down, and I have authority to take it again" (10:17–18). Satan, a king whose hellish hordes put his subjects through the torments of death even in life: "they will seek death and not find it; they will long to die but death will flee from them" (Revelation 9:6)—yet they will die even though they live. Jesus, the king who gives his subjects life even in death: "The one believing in me will live even though he dies" (John 11:25). The kingdom of love over against a kingdom of hate; of unity, "one flock" under "one shepherd" (John 10:16), over against a fractiousness in which difference spells deadly conflict: "With hatred, the ten horns you saw on the beast [the beast that supports the harlot] will turn against the harlot . . . devour her flesh and set her on fire," that is, the harlot Babylon who sits "enthroned [over] peoples and crowds and nations and tongues" (Revelation 17:15–16).

For Christians, then, the teaching of different languages signifies salvation from the divisive judgment at Babel, a recapturing through Christ of the unity of human beings, this time not by the hubris of making a name for ourselves by building a tower that reaches to heaven, but by joining that one who, because he came down from heaven, was lifted back up by way of a cross that he might draw to himself all—speakers of Aramaic, Latin, Greek, and any other language deriving from Babel. For there's no "and" to introduce the last language that John lists. I made a mistake in my title. I wasn't reading the text carefully enough, but allowed myself to be influenced by the many English translations that without ancient textual support insert "and." Not "Aramaic, Latin, *and* Greek"; rather, "Aramaic, Latin, Greek." There's no sense of closure. The list remains open-ended. For God loved the world in this way, by lifting up his Son so high that regardless of language, nobody would fall outside the field of Jesus' attractive power.

And thus we read in John's blessed apocalyptic vision, "I looked, and behold, a great crowd, whom no one could number, from every nation and [all] tribes and peoples— *and tongues*—standing before the throne and before the Lamb, clothed in white robes, and palm branches in their hands, and shouting with a loud voice saying, 'Salvation to our God who sits on the throne and to the Lamb!'" (Revelation 7:9–10). Here's a vision that sets forth, not the reversal of Babel, but its redemption, so that we'll not be reduced to a single heavenly language—be it Aramaic, Latin, Greek, or any other language. Rather, I suspect all God's people will become multilingual. Better than that— *omni*lingual! And so our present work of teaching foreign languages turns into a bit of realized eschatology anticipating that day. Amen.

Part Three:

Controversial Talks

Inspiration, Inerrancy, and Apparent Discrepancies in the Gospels

~ Delivered to alumni in a Homecoming class ~

My recently published commentary on Matthew has raised questions about biblical inspiration and inerrancy in relation to apparent discrepancies in the Gospels.* So this talk won't give an objective survey of the topic—rather, a personal statement of my own position. I'll begin, however, with a review of some traditionally evangelical Christian beliefs about the Bible.

The Bible is inspired; that is, the Spirit of God so supervised its human authors that what they wrote there is God's authoritative Word to us. The Bible is verbally inspired; that is, the Holy Spirit inspired the very words of Scripture, not just the concepts behind the words. Biblical inspiration is also plenary; that is, the whole Bible is inspired, not just parts of it. As a result of such inspiration, the Bible is inerrant. Evangelical Christians hold these beliefs about the Bible (though some prefer the term "infallible" over the term "inerrant"). As an evangelical Christian, I hold them.

Recently a debate has arisen among evangelical Christians regarding the inerrancy of the Bible. Some of them have argued that the term "inerrancy" should be given up, because it raises false expectations with regard to historical and scientific precision, because it doesn't leave enough

*Robert H. Gundry, *Matthew: A Commentary on His Literary and Theological Art* (Grand Rapids: Eerdmans, 1982). The second, revised edition (1994) has extensive supplements and a new subtitle, *A Commentary on His Handbook for a Mixed Church under Persecution*, and though out of print is available by print-on-demand.

room in most people's minds for the different kinds of literature that appear in the Bible, and because it therefore has to be qualified too much. Other evangelicals argue that it's better to qualify the term "inerrancy" than to give it up, because giving it up would leave a false impression that biblical authority is being given up as well. I take the view that we ought to keep the term.

Now another question arises: What is the meaning of inerrancy? In other words, what are the standards for saying something is errant or inerrant? If I say, "Just a second," when I'm shaving and my wife calls me for breakfast yet it takes me a minute or so to get to the breakfast table, nobody accuses me of speaking error. But if I say, "Just a second," during a missile launch at Vandenberg Air Force Base and it turns out to be a minute or so, I'll rightly be accused of speaking error. A different intention, suitable to a different setting, makes the difference even though the words are the same.

But how far can we go with this kind of reasoning? Can we also say the Bible makes up things on the printed page that never really happened in history? The answer has to be yes. Consider the parables. For example, "A certain man went down from Jerusalem to Jericho." A person would hardly be accused of denying the doctrine of biblical inerrancy because he denies that the parable of the good Samaritan is a historical report even though the parable begins and continues just the way a historical report would begin and continue and even though the scriptural text never uses the term "parable" for this story. We believe that Jesus *told* the parable in history, but we don't have to believe that *what* he told happened in history. Similarly with other parables. Now the question becomes interesting. If some parables, including ones not described as parables, look like historical reports but aren't, is it possible that other parts of the Bible may look like historical reports but not be such? Or if they aren't entirely unhistorical, might they be partly historical and partly unhistorical, containing a lot of history but some literary creativity too?

How do we decide such a question? Because of the parables we can't deny the possibility of unhistorical elements in the Bible. And it would be unfair to let our prejudices determine in advance the answer to our question concerning other parts of the Bible. There are two ways to answer the question fairly: (1) we must look at the kinds of writing Jews in the first century were used to, because the first Christians—in particular, most if not all the writers of the New Testament—were Jewish; (2) we should look for indications in the Bible itself, and here I will stress Matthew in comparison with Mark and Luke.

Take the writings to which first-century Jews were accustomed, beginning with their own Old Testament. As even the strictest inerrantists recognize, the early genealogies in Genesis contain gaps of thousands of years. In other words, they aren't the straightforward lists of ancestors, generation by generation, that we usually think of as constituting a genealogy. The first two chapters of Judges indicate that the nation of Israel didn't conquer the land of Canaan completely, not by a long shot. They do much better in Joshua 1–12. That is to say, the book of Joshua appears to give an idealized picture, whereas the book of Judges gives a historically more realistic picture. Similarly, the book of Chronicles idealizes David, whereas Samuel-Kings gives a historically more realistic portrait, warts and all. Apparently the idealistic accounts I've just referred to weren't intended to be taken as purely historical reports. They were intended to portray what *should* have been in the past and what *will* be in the future.

Likewise in Jewish literature written after the close of the Old Testament and up through the time of the New Testament, various authors took liberties with the data of the Old Testament. Where the text of Genesis has only God's command that Abraham take a journey throughout the promised land, one author creates a whole journey in order to make Abraham a good example of obedience. The author even details the particular places that Abraham visited. The first-century Jewish historian Josephus includes stories about Moses' boyhood that we have no reason to think had any historical basis. He even makes the grownup Moses into the general of the Egyptian army who leads them out to defeat a horde of Ethiopians. To avoid a bad example of lying, another Jewish author changes Jacob's false statement to his father Isaac, "I am Esau," into the truthful statement, "I am your son." Yet another Jewish author of the period does what many a modern preacher does but what the biblical text doesn't mention at all: he makes Isaac offer himself willingly when Abraham starts to sacrifice him at God's command.

In fact, these and other ancient Jewish authors were doing what practically every contemporary evangelical does in handling the biblical text. They were dressing it up here, changing it there, updating it in another passage, inserting an imaginary conversation or event or detail in yet another passage—all to make the text more applicable, more emphatic, more contemporary. Think of present-day preachers who've made Daniel so trustful in the lions' den that he slept on a lion's mane all night, or who've made up whole conversations between the serpent and Adam and Eve in the Garden of Eden or between the Devil and Jesus in the temptation stories. Unless these changes and additions contradict some doctrine taught in the Bible, nobody accuses these preachers of making mistakes or speaking errors. No, everybody understands that they're taking sermonic liberties well accepted as a legitimate mode of communication.

But somebody will say that contemporary preachers aren't inspired, whereas the Bible is different. It *is* inspired. Therefore it can't contain this mode of communication. When the Bible says something happened in such and such a way, it happened. And it happened just that way. This kind of comment overlooks, however, that there may be a difference between something's happening in a story and something's happening in history. Remember, the parables show that not everything which happened on the pages of the Bible happened in history. If taking liberties in a sermon is a legitimate mode of communication, there is nothing wrong with taking liberties in some parts of the Bible, because biblical authors use a wide range of literary modes: not only fiction in parables that would be misleading if taken as historical reports, but also apocalyptic symbols that would be misleading if taken as literalistic language, proverbs that would be misleading if taken as rules that have no exceptions, love-poetry that would be misleading if taken as prose, and so on and on.

Do we have evidence that Matthew took liberties with historical data in a way similar to the way contemporary preachers take sermonic liberties with scriptural data? Again the answer has to be yes. Take the very first passage in Matthew, the genealogy of Jesus (1:1–17). Matthew divides it into three sets of fourteen generations each. Yet the corresponding genealogies in the Old Testament (which is also inspired!) show that Matthew deliberately skips four generations to get his numerical scheme (see 1 Chronicles 3), so that his phrase "*all* the generations" must mean all the generations in his list, not all the generations in history. The least we can say is that he isn't writing the way we would demand a modern genealogist to write. Later in his Gospel, he has Jesus cleanse the temple on the same day Jesus rides into Jerusalem (21:1–18), whereas Mark writes that the cleansing of the temple takes place the next day (11:1–18). Similarly, Matthew has the fig tree that Jesus cursed wither up as soon as Jesus curses it, on the spot, while his disciples are looking on (21:18–20). In Mark the fig tree withers up over the course of a day, and the withering isn't noticed till the next day (11:12–14, 20–21). Matthew has Peter denying Jesus at different locations in the palace of the high priest and under pressure from different people as compared with the locations and people mentioned in the corresponding passages in Mark and Luke (compare, for example, the accounts of the second denial in Matthew 26:71–72; Mark 14:69–70a; Luke 22:58).

We're dealing not only with isolated instances of apparent discrepancy. Throughout the Gospel of Matthew the disciples look much more knowledgeable than they do in Mark, where they constantly look stupid. For example, at the end of one story in Mark Jesus asks the disciples, "Don't you understand yet?" (8:21). But Matthew concludes the corresponding paragraph in his Gospel with the comment, "Then the disciples understood . . ." (16:12). Instead of giving a historically realistic picture of the disciples here and elsewhere, he idealizes them to make them an example of what his Christian audience should be, namely, disciples who know and understand the teaching and example of Jesus much better than the original disciples actually did in history. The artificial scheme of three sets of fourteen generations each is designed to portray Jesus as the greater Son of David, the numerical equivalent of whose Hebrew name is fourteen. Matthew advances the cleansing of the temple and the withering of the fig tree, not to falsify history, but to emphasize the theological point that God is displeased with the Jewish leaders who rejected Jesus.

There are two ways of harmonizing apparent discrepancies. One is to insist that everything is historical and figure out some way that everything can be historical at once. For example, I used to say in regard to the withering of the fig tree that Matthew was writing topically rather than chronologically. Then I opened my eyes wide enough to see that Matthew uses a chronological word. Twice he says that the fig tree withered "immediately" even though elsewhere in his Gospel he usually deletes the notion of immediacy as compared with Mark. A classic way of harmonizing the apparent discrepancies concerning Peter's denials of Jesus is to say that Peter denied Jesus more than three times, say, four, six, or even eight times. But such harmonizations run into trouble when we remember that Jesus predicted three denials, and that after the resurrection he had Peter affirm his love for him three times—not four, six, or eight times (John 21:15–19; compare the three times a sheet was let down in Peter's vision at Acts 10:9–16). In other words, this way of harmonizing the apparent discrepancies often and unwittingly does damage to verbal inspiration because it doesn't allow the words of Scripture to be taken in their natural sense.

The other way to harmonize these apparent discrepancies is to say that Matthew (he's my example) doesn't intend to write a purely historical report even though a great deal of history comes through in his Gospel. He intends to write a

Gospel more in the fashion that evangelical preachers adopt in preaching sermons. So if he takes the kinds of liberties contemporary preachers take, we should accuse him of writing error no more than we accuse contemporary preachers of speaking error. We can relax. Matthew is using a perfectly acceptable mode of communication. The discrepancies aren't problems any more. They're just liberties, and the theological points they make are just as theologically inerrant as statements intended to be taken as historical are historically inerrant.

Scholars can distinguish which way Matthew intends to speak by comparing his text with that of the other Gospels and with the style of Jewish literature in use during the first century. But the effect of this scholarly effort is to give the Bible back to lay people. It's written for lay people anyway. They don't need to read the Bible with a magnifying glass the way a scholar does. They don't need to get tangled up in comparing the Gospels to find out where Peter was when he denied Jesus the second time and who challenged him, or what day of the week it was when Jesus cleansed the temple and the fig tree withered and how much the disciples understood or didn't understand. The Gospels were written the way preachers preach, not the way scholars do research. So let the Gospels be read the way sermons are listened to.

Sometimes a sermon is careful and exact, sometimes free and creative. Preachers and audiences swing from one to the other without a second thought. And there are many different degrees of exactitude and creativity. But we accept them all for what they are, so long as they are well done. Inspiration and inerrancy don't rule out creativity any more than they demand scientific precision. Inspiration and inerrancy just mean that whatever kind of writing we find at any point in the Bible, it is perfectly well done. So we should take it however it is meant to be taken, not in a way it isn't meant to be taken. If we read the Bible this way, we'll be more biblical. If we don't, but impose on the Bible what we think should have been intended, we'll be less biblical even in our attempt to defend it. I'd rather be more biblical.

Some Exegetical Notes on Divorce and Remarriage in Scripture

~ Delivered in a seminar for faculty ~

Deuteronomy 24:1–4 did not prescribe divorce and remarriage, but only treated it as an existing practice and prohibited a man's remarrying the same woman if she had been another man's wife in the meantime. This prohibition had the effect of discouraging divorce by making the husband realize that if he divorced his wife and she remarried he could never get her back again even though her next husband died or divorced her (compare Jeremiah 3:1). Though divorce and remarriage were presupposed and therefore allowed (because of hardheartedness, according to Jesus [Mark 10:5; Matthew 19:8]), the Mosaic legislation did not approve divorce and remarriage but purposed to reduce it; and Malachi 2:16 quotes "the LORD, the God of Israel" as saying, "I hate divorce."

Jesus takes the Mosaic legislation further in the same direction by teaching a higher standard for the new age. Luke 16:18 says absolutely—that is, without exception—not only that getting divorced and remarried constitutes adultery but also that a person who has never previously been married commits adultery by marrying a divorced person.

Mark 10:1–12 (especially verses 9, 11–12) prohibits divorce and says that remarriage constitutes adultery.

Matthew 5:31–32 allows divorce for *porneia*. Elsewhere in ancient Greek literature *porneia* is a general term for sexual immorality, most often in connection with prostitution but also in reference to other kinds of illicit sexual unions (such as incest, premarital sex, adultery [which is sex with someone else's spouse or someone not your own spouse], etc.). But instead of making *porneia* an exception for remarriage as well as for divorce, Matthew 5:31–32 says that marrying a divorced person constitutes adultery (see Luke 16:18 again).

Matthew 19:1–12 also mentions the exception for *porneia*. Many (perhaps most) scholars think it applies here to remarriage as well as to divorce. The phrase "except for *porneia*" occurs right after the mention of divorce, however, so that it may refer only to divorce rather than also to remarriage, which is mentioned next; and there are several reasons *not* to take the phrase as applying additionally to remarriage: (1) The disciples' reaction that the strictness of what Jesus has just said makes it better not to marry at all (verse 10) is easier to understand if they understood him to be making no exception for remarriage, but only for divorce. (2) Jesus' answering in terms of "eunuchs who have made themselves eunuchs for the sake of the kingdom of heaven" (verses 11–12) has no clear relation to the preceding context if we think literally of castration, and therefore appears to symbolize denying oneself the sexual benefit of remarriage if a divorce has taken place; that is to say, eunuchry stands for staying single. (3) Jesus' statement that most people find this standard intolerable favors that he is not allowing remarriage even under the exception that allows divorce. (4) His additional statement that this word "has been given" to the disciples (verse 11b) recalls the phraseology of 13:11, which says that the mysteries of the kingdom of heaven "have been given" to the disciples, but not to nondisciples. This recollection favors that "the one who is able to accept" Jesus' obligatory word on living as a eunuch (19:12d) is any divorced disciple as opposed to a divorced nondisciple, not a person with the ability to stay single as opposed to the person who supposedly cannot get along without marriage. In other words, just as the giving of the mysteries to the disciples enables them to live in the kingdom, so the giving of Jesus' word on eunuchs enables the disciples to obey his prohibition of remarriage. (5) The fact that Matthew's Gospel is the only one to relate the disciples' surprise at the strictness of Jesus' teaching and is also the only one to mention living as a eunuch makes it look as though Matthew is going out of his way to keep his readers from thinking that "except for *porneia*" applies to remarriage.

The undisputed application of the exception to divorce in both Matthew 5:32 and 19:9 rules out divorce for another reason and later using the remarriage of one's ex-spouse as an out for one's own remarriage to someone else. *Porneia* has to be the ground of the divorce whether or not remarriage is allowable.

Does conversion give a new start, so that a person who was divorced before conversion may scripturally remarry afterwards? No, because Jesus addresses his teaching to the Pharisees, who are nondisciples, as well as to his disciples (Luke 16:14; Mark 10:2; Matthew 19:3). Private elaboration to his disciples does not negate the initial address to nondisciples.

Sometimes it is said that Jesus' teaching sets out an idealistic standard toward which we are to aim, but that God's grace covers our failures to attain this standard (failures that are inevitable in the present overlap of the evil age and the age of salvation) and allows us to try again. God's grace certainly covers our failures, but where is the evidence that it allows us to try again in remarriage? On the contrary, Matthew brings his Gospel to a climax with Jesus' call to teach the keeping of all his commandments during the present age (28:20); and, as we have seen, the condemnation of remarriage as adultery figures twice among those commandments (5:32; 19:9). Furthermore, Jesus' teaching on this topic has the distinction of being the only moral commandment of his that the apostle Paul explicitly quotes and applies to Christian conduct in the present age (1 Corinthians 7:10–11). If a person does remarry, will God's grace take care of that disobedience, too? Presumably so, if there is repentance and faith. But we do not use grace as a reason to go ahead and disobey commandments. To do so would be to sin that grace may abound, against which Paul recoils in horror (Romans 6:1–2).

1 Corinthians 7:10–11 discourages but allows the breakup of Christian couples, but it prohibits remarriage and urges reconciliation. 1 Corinthians 7:13 commands a Christian with a non-Christian spouse (apparently they were married before one of them converted) to maintain the marriage if the non-Christian is willing. 1 Corinthians 7:15 says, however, that the Christian is not "under bondage" if the non-Christian dissolves the marriage. Some people argue that if being "bound" in verse 39 means being *un*free to remarry, then *not* being under bondage in verse 15 must mean being free to remarry. But the Greek word in verse 15 is *dedoulôtai*, which means "enslaved," whereas the Greek word in verse 39 is *dedetai*, which is completely different and means "bound" in the sense of being "tied up." Of course, different Greek words may express the same thought; but here we have reasons to doubt sameness of meaning: (1) If verse 15 allowed remarriage before the death of the first spouse it would contradict verse 39, which says that only death can break the marriage bond. (2) The immediate context of verse 15 deals with the question of maintaining a first marriage, not with the possibility of a second marriage. (3) The last clause in verse 15 ("but God has called us to peace") seems to

interpret "not under bondage" earlier in the verse, not as freedom to remarry, but as freedom from the obligation of trying to maintain the original marriage against the wish of the non-Christian spouse to dissolve it.

Paul begins a new topic in 1 Corinthians 7:25 ("Now concerning virgins"). Therefore his statements in verse 28 ("but if you [a man] should marry, you have not sinned; and if a virgin should marry, she has not sinned") have nothing to do with divorce and remarriage. Paul is addressing Christians who have never been married before but who are contemplating marriage to someone in the same state. He is also addressing widows and widowers, who may legitimately contemplate another marriage (as shown by the similarity of the contrast in verse 27 between being 'bound" and being "released" and the contrast in verse 39 between being "bound" [the same Greek word] and being "free" to get married again because the first spouse "is dead").

Romans 7:1–3 uses the law that remarriage after divorce constitutes adultery as an illustration. An exception on remarriage is not mentioned, and it would weaken the illustration considerably. Though this argument is not so strong as it would be if Paul were teaching directly on divorce and remarriage, it certainly supports what other passages teach.

An Unexegetical Postscript

Some people may reason that the foregoing exegetical points must be wrong because the loving God of the Bible wants his human creatures to be happy and therefore would not deny divorced people another chance for marital happiness, especially if they were non-Christians when they divorced or were the innocent party. Several things need to be said about this way of thinking: (1) It may prove too much, for it could lead to an endless succession of new chances for marital happiness no matter how many previous attempts failed. It provides no reason to halt after the failure of the second or third (or fifth or tenth) attempt. (A prominent Christian leader, himself divorced and remarried, once told me that an innocent party like him would be free to remarry twenty times, that is, without limit.) (2) It falsely makes human happiness the determinative criterion of what God considers right. (3) It overvalues the ability of human beings to predict what will make them happy (consider the higher rate of divorce among remarried people). (4) It allows a human definition of God's love to overturn the natural meaning of Scripture, which ought to determine our concept of his love. (5) It takes an individually narrow view based on an opinion of what will make one or two persons happy. For everybody thinks there is too much divorce and remarriage in general, but nearly everybody thinks he himself or she herself or a relative or a close friend has good reason to divorce and remarry as an exception to the general rule. Everybody who wants to divorce and remarry is someone's close friend or relative or a self, however. So everybody who wants to divorce and remarry turns out to be an exception to the general rule against divorce and remarriage. As a result, the basic unit of society—the family—falls apart throughout the whole of society, as has in fact happened. This social disaster then rebounds to produce individual disasters. Not only do children lose the security of stable families, with an endless train of sad consequences; but also spouses lose even in their first marriage the security that marriage used to provide. Ironically, what started out as an allowance for a relatively few divorced people to find happiness in a new marriage ends up robbing a far larger number of people of happiness right from the start.

On Homosex* and
Homosexual Marriage

*~ Delivered in response to comments
in a student newspaper ~*

All biblically literate discussants recognize three facts: (1) the Bible never puts homosex of any kind in a favorable light; (2) homosex always appears in association with evil; and (3) everywhere an explicit judgment is rendered we have a condemnation or a prohibition. So what arguments, exegetical and hermeneutical, do some Christians adduce for accepting homosex at least in a single committed relationship—or in marriage, if homosexual marriage were to be legalized? I'll put those arguments in the form of italicized questions, and add comments and counter questions in roman type.

Don't the biblical condemnations and prohibitions consist in a few isolated prooftexts as opposed to the larger and therefore weightier emphases on compassionate love and equal justice? No, for a variety of reasons:

First, that line of argument would lead to accepting incest and bestiality; for they get less bad press in the Bible than homosex does.

Second, the Bible pays more attention to homosex than is sometimes thought: three and perhaps four passages in the Pentateuch,** one in the Historical Books,° probably three in the Prophets,°° at least three, probably five and possibly

---

* "Homosex" is shorthand for engaging in homosexual intercourse.

** Genesis 9:20–27 (perhaps); 19:4–11; Leviticus 18:22; 20:13.

° Judges 19:22–26.

°° Ezekiel 16:50; 18:12; 33:26.

ten, in the Epistles,* not to count up references to homosexual cultic and noncultic prostitution.**

Third, Paul's citing both female and male homosex as prime examples of dishonorable passions (Romans 1:24–27, where he doesn't even mention fornication and adultery) and stating that neither passive nor active gays will inherit God's kingdom (1 Corinthians 6:9) show the gravity of this sin.

Fourth, far from offering an isolated prooftext, Paul puts his condemnation of homosex squarely in the large theological framework of God's creation (Romans 1:18–32). Specifically, Paul's description of homosex as "against nature" has to do with God as "Creator" making human "bodies" as "male" and "female" for the sexual "use" of each other—all in verbal and conceptual allusion to Genesis 1:26–28.

And fifth, what counts as Christian love and justice needs definition according to biblical commands and prohibitions; and Scripture prohibits homosex. The care and love of pedophiles for children, which can be genuine (and often *has* been), doesn't usually lead Christians who accept homosex between loving, caring adults to condone pederasty, not even when the youngster consents to, seeks after, and benefits from a pederastic relationship (as has

* Romans 1:24–27; 1 Corinthians 6:9–11; 1 Timothy 1:10; 2 Peter 2:7 (probably); Jude 7 (probably). And since Paul clearly associates "uncleanness" with homosex in Romans 1:24–27, he may well mean homosex when writing "uncleanness" in 2 Corinthians 12:21; Galatians 5:19; Ephesians 4:19; 5:3, 5; Colossians 3:5, in which passages the term occurs alongside "fornication" (whose most common meaning has to do with visiting prostitutes), "debauchery," "passion," and "evil desire."

**As compared with references to fornication and adultery, the *relative* fewness of references to homosex is almost certainly due to the lower incidence of homosex.

often happened). Allow love in general to trump specific biblical guidelines and you leave little or no theological reason to limit homo- or heterosex to a single committed relationship. In fact, at a meeting celebrating the tenth anniversary of the Reimagining God conference, the argument was made that we might well spread love around by engaging multiple sexual partners.

But isn't it unfair for a person of homosexual orientation not to have even a hope of sexual fulfillment? Well, then, should we allow those of pedophilic and necrophilic orientations to carry out *their* sexual proclivities? One could think of other proclivities, both sexual and nonsexual, whose fulfillment both the Bible and society at large disallow. And what of the spouse whose bride or groom has been sexually incapacitated—permanently—in an auto accident on the way from wedding ceremony to bridal chamber? (I know firsthand an actual case very like that.) Should the lack of hope for sexual fulfillment in that marriage free the spouse to visit prostitutes, take a paramour, or divorce the incapacitated spouse and remarry?

But in view of Jesus' silence on homosex and the command, "Judge not that you not be judged" (Matthew 7:1), shouldn't we welcome homosexuals just as he welcomed sinners and prostitutes? Yes; but he didn't tolerate, much less approve, their sinning and prostitution. Instead, he called them to repentance. Furthermore, his pronouncements on sexual conduct display greater-than-usual strictness, not greater-than-usual lenience (see especially Matthew 5:27–30; Luke 16:18); and his positive comments, like Paul's, are limited to heterosex within marriage (for example, Mark 10:1–9). So we can hardly use his silence on homosex, welcoming of sinners, and emphasis on the love-command for toleration or approval of homosex in the Christian community any more than we can, or do, use them to tolerate or approve prostitution, adultery, incest, bestiality, and necrophilism, on the last three of which he was likewise silent. Besides, Christians don't restrict scriptural authority to the quoted words of Jesus.

Yet doesn't the church need to accept into Christian fellowship practicing homosexuals in a single committed relationship just as the early church had to accept uncircumcised and therefore ritually impure Gentiles? No, because divine revelation, recorded in Scripture, orders the acceptance of such Gentiles, whereas nothing in Scripture orders churchly acceptance of practicing homosexuals. On the contrary, Paul cites homosex as an egregious example of immorality and commands Christians "not to associate or even eat with any so-called brother or sister who is immoral," though he does allow them to associate with evildoers of all sorts who make no profession of Christian faith (otherwise, "you would have to go out of the world" [1 Corinthians 5:9–11]).* And Scripture rescinds dietary and other ritual laws but maintains the prohibition of homosex. What Christian would justify child sacrifice, incest, adultery, and bestiality on the ground that their prohibition, like that of homosex, occurs in the vicinity of the now rescinded Levitical laws of ritual purity? Increasingly, then, Christians who accept homosex are frankly denying the authority of the Bible at least on this matter (and usually on other matters too).

* In view of the context of a man's living with his father's wife, "such as not even the Gentiles do" (1 Corinthians 5:1), Paul must have in mind ongoing or serial immorality of an unrepentant sort, not a moral lapse that occasions repentance.

Well, then, might the biblical proscription of homosex be limited to pederasty, promiscuity, rape, cult prostitution, and—in general—exploitation by males? No. Homosexual rape appears in the story of Sodom and Judges 19—perhaps also in the story of Noah's drunkenness—and homosexual cult prostitution often gets mentioned. But the remaining condemnations show no signs of any limitation. For example, the Greek language has perfectly good nouns for a pederast (*paiderastês*) and pederasty (*paiderastia*), plus a cognate verb (*paiderasteô*). None of them appear in the New Testament to suggest a limitation to pederasty, and by New Testament times pederasty had declined while other forms of homosex continued unabated. Whatever its form, homosex always appears in the Bible to be *as such* a parade example of promiscuity; and neither Greco-Roman nor Jewish literature of the period limits homosex to pederasty, promiscuity, rape, and cult prostitution.

Moreover, Leviticus 20:13 prescribes capital punishment for the passive as well as active partner in homosex. 1 Corinthians 6:9 delays punishment till the end, excludes gays from God's kingdom, and mentions passive partners ahead of active ones. And Romans 1:26 pairs lesbians with gays and mentions the lesbians first (even though no other literature of the period mentions lesbianism before gayism), so that we shouldn't consider exploitation by males a limiting factor. Paul's expression, "burning in their desire toward one another" (Romans 1:27), puts passive and active gays under the same blanket of condemnation. (Note that the New Testament's delaying of the Levitical death penalty for adultery and incest till the Last Judgment leads hardly anyone to accept adultery and incest.)

Shouldn't we treat the biblical prohibition of homosex as a cultural artifact to be discarded, however, just as we've discarded as a cultural artifact biblical statements about slavery? No, because though the Bible doesn't condemn slavery, it doesn't command slavery; and it makes slavery inconsequential (Galatians 3:28) but doesn't make homosex inconsequential. Quite the reverse!

But biblical writers weren't aware of homosexual orientation, were they? Didn't they falsely assume that everybody is heterosexual and therefore commits homosexual acts against his or her nature, whereas we know better? No, for as a matter of fact ancient literature displays a recognition that some people are homosexually oriented, as distinct from bi- and heterosexuals who engage in homosex, and offers possible explanations—from nature to nurture—for homosexual orientation. Indeed, this literature also knows of consensual, adult, and even exclusive, lifelong homosexual unions. Furthermore, Paul's basing the condemnation of homosex on God's creation of human beings as male and female "bodies" (Romans 1:24–27), that is, as anatomically fitted to each other, makes a homosexual orientation—whatever its cause or causes—irrelevant to the condemnation.

Doesn't the Bible prohibit homosex, however, only because it degrades male honor by making a male function as a passive female or by a female's usurping the active function of a male? That rationale does appear in ancient literature outside the Bible.* But one looks in vain for it inside the Bible. Rather, the prohibition springs from God's creation of male and female as complementary *co*rulers of the earth. Moreover, why not tolerate adultery now that we no longer consider it an affront to male honor

* For references to extrabiblical ancient literature on this and foregoing points, see the writings of Gagnon and Smith listed below in the Select Bibliography.

and a theft of male property (another man's wife), as it used to be considered? The Paul who condemns homosex is the same Paul who writes that a wife has sexual authority over her husband's body, just as vice versa (1 Corinthians 7:3–4). So much for male honor in the matter of sex!

Doesn't the Bible disapprove of homosex because the waste of seed contravenes God's command to replenish the earth, whereas we now have the problem of over-population and accept contraception? No, because the Bible prohibits fornication, incest, and adultery even though they *are* procreative; and it doesn't prohibit having sex with your pregnant wife even though it wastes seed.

But if Christians can violate biblical teachings on pacifism and on divorce-plus-remarriage, and be accepted in the church, why can't they violate the biblical proscription of homosex and be accepted in the church? Well, two wrongs don't make a right. Besides, there's a legitimate debate whether the Bible teaches pacifism in international relations and enforcement of law, or only in Christians' reaction to persecution for the faith. Most importantly, the Bible seeks to limit or end the cycle of divorce-plus-remarriage, not bless it, as some are advocating Christians do for homosex.

Why single out homosex for special condemnation when the Bible condemns other sins, such as self-righteousness and pride, at least as much. It isn't that those opposed to homosex are singling it out for special condemnation. It's that those wanting to make homosex acceptable are singling it out for special recommendation, or at least for special toleration. As for the comparison with self-righteousness and pride, they are attitudinal sins whose prohibition neither the church nor society at large can enforce, whereas the prohibition of homosex is enforceable. We could equally well ask why murder should be singled out for special condemnation when the Bible condemns other sins, such as self-righteousness and pride, at least as much. The answer is the same: society can enforce the prohibition of murder but not that of self-righteousness and pride. We have to leave the judgment of self-righteousness and pride to God.

No heterosexual marriage attains to God's ideal, does it, but in a more or less limited way is blessed by God, isn't it? Likewise a homosexual union doesn't attain to God's ideal, but in a more or less limited way may be blessed by God, can't it (compare polygamy and concubinage in the Old Testament)? No, because homosex is divinely prohibited, whereas marriage was divinely instituted. So there's no analogy to be drawn between marriage and a homosexual union. Even if there were, we surely wouldn't say that sex with a prostitute, our neighbor's spouse, a beast, or a corpse doesn't attain to God's ideal but in a more or less limited way may be blessed by God. And in view of the severity with which Scripture condemns homosex, we can hardly think that it falls less short of God's ideal than these other kinds of immoral sex that few would dare to say are God-blessed *at all.*

But how can we deny that some practicing homosexuals exhibit the fruit of the Spirit ("love, joy, peace [and so on]" [Galatians 5:22–23])? We *can* deny it, indeed we *must* deny it; for the immediately surrounding passage (1) excludes from God's kingdom those who practice (among other evils) "sexual immorality" and "sensuality"; (2) declares that "those who belong to Christ Jesus have crucified the flesh with its passions and desires"; and (3) says that those who "walk by the Spirit . . . will not carry out the desire of the flesh" (Galatians 5:16–21, 24). After all, the last-listed fruit of the Spirit is "self-control," which elsewhere in Paul has special reference to sexual behavior (1 Corinthians 7:9; 9:25*).

A thorough discussion would take up pastoral questions of how to help professing Christians who struggle with their sexual proclivities (of whatever sort they might be) and how to induce necessary reform in sexual behavior. Such a discussion would also propose an anti-homosex rationale that would make sense to non-Christians. That kind of rationale couldn't appeal to biblical authority; but because human culture differs from one time and place to another time and place, the search for a universal secular rationale—apart from a Pauline-like appeal to the configuration of male and female bodies—is liable to prove futile. There was a time and place, for example, when one could argue more or less convincingly for the exclusivity of heterosex within marriage on the grounds that males need the civilizing influence of a wife, that wives need a husband's protection, and that children need the stable rearing provided by a husband and wife. The argument may still possess validity; but in an age of feminism, high rates of divorce and singleness, and daycare centers for children, that argument has lost much of its force. It remains to be seen whether psychologists, sociologists, and medical doctors can do better in our present setting.

Finally, then, why are Christians debating the homosexual issue, including homosexual marriage? Answer: because against twenty centuries of churchly understanding of

---

* This latter reference has to do with the self-control required for athletic competition. It included ten months of abstinence from sexual intercourse.

179

scriptural teaching on homosex, some Christians—mainly in the increasingly worldly church of the western northern hemisphere—are redefining homosex as not-sin but aren't redefining similarly other behaviors, such as adultery and pederasty, as not-sin. And they are redefining homosex as not-sin both to the horror of almost all Christians throughout the rest of the world (the two-thirds world of multiculturalism and global Christianity) and with a dubious claim to know the mind of the Spirit better than the biblical authors did. If some Christians were to start redefining behaviors such as adultery and pederasty as not-sin, we would be debating those issues too.

Select Bibliography:

Gagnon, Robert A. J. *The Bible and Homosexual Practice: Texts and Hermeneutics*. Nashville: Abingdon Press, 2001. (A thorough discussion opposed to acceptance of homosex)

Holben, L. R. *What Christians Think about Homosexuality: Six Representative Viewpoints*. North Richland Hills, Tex.: BIBAL Press, 1999. (Written by a homosexual who attempts to catalog different views and arguments objectively)

Homosexuality, Science, and the "Plain Sense" of Scripture. Ed. David L. Balch. Grand Rapids: Eerdmans Publishing Company, 2000. (Essays by various authors advocating different views)

Smith, Mark D. "Ancient Bisexuality and the Interpretation of Romans 1:26–27," *Journal of the American Academy of Religion*, 64 (1996): 223–56. (An essay by an ancient historian who falsifies a number of claims made in behalf of homosex on the basis of ancient practice)

See also the periodical *Christian Century*, June 5–12 (2002): 32–34 and August 14–17 (2002): 40–44, for a vigorous exchange between Gagnon and Walter Wink, a leading proponent of Christian acceptance of homosex.

The Hopelessness of the Unevangelized

~ Delivered in a seminar for faculty ~

Lately there has come out of cold storage a question that has been hibernating among conservative evangelicals for some time. That question has to do with the status of people who live and die without ever hearing the gospel of Jesus Christ. Will God consign them to everlasting punishment? If so, where is his sense of fair play—they never had a chance—let alone his love for them? If not, through what means and at what time does he give them opportunity to be saved?

This question of theodicy (divine justice) needs open discussion. We can easily identify reasons for its acuteness: (1) the relative fewness of the saved under the traditional view that apart from evangelization in their lifetimes people have no hope (compare Luke 13:23, "Lord, are there few who are being saved?" and the whole book of *4 Ezra*); (2) the guilt of Christians in failing to evangelize them; and (3) the eternality of punishment in the hereafter. These considerations have always troubled pious minds.

In recent times historical factors have heightened sensitivity to the question. The downfall of monarchism and the rise of egalitarianism in the political realm have made it hard for people to continue thinking of God as a king who exercises his sovereignty at what surely looks to be the outrageous expense of vast hordes of humanity. Add the lingering myths of the happy heathen and the noble savage; the modern syndrome of self-pity, evident in the anti-heroes of literature, drama, and cinema and in the attribution of human failings to genetic and environmental factors; the current emphasis on love without holiness, on tolerance without convictions; the exchange of "convictions" (connoting objective truths) for mere "values" (connoting subjective preferences); and the cosmopolitanism of the global village, in which people all over the world have a more immediate awareness of one another than they ever had before. This mixture offers a witches' brew to anyone who would dare defend the traditional view, which sat a little less uncomfortably in provincial society.

Let us rule out the doctrines of universal salvation and of the annihilation of the wicked (also called conditional immortality). The former solves our problem by positing the salvation of all people in the end but runs aground on texts that describe the eternal punishment of unbelievers (see, for example, Matthew 25:46; Revelation 14:11; 20:10, 15) and on Jesus' explicit statements—in the Sermon on the Mount of all places!—that "wide is the gate and broad the way leading to destruction, and *many* are the ones who enter through it" and "how narrow is the gate and confined the road leading to life, and *few* are the ones who find it" (Matthew 7:13–14). The reconciliation of all things (Ephesians 1:10; Colossians 1:19–20) refers to the new creation in Christ (Ephesians 1:22–23; Colossians 1:17–18), outside of which fall the unsaved (see Ephesians 2:3; 5:5–6; Colossians 3:5–6, 12 [noting that the initial "e" in "elect" indicates a choice of some "out of" a larger number (so also the original Greek)]; and Revelation 21:8). In view of the contrast between "those who are being saved" and "those who are perishing" in 2 Corinthians 2:14–16, the reconciling of "the world" to God in 5:19 cannot imply universal salvation as a coming actuality, or even as a possibility—rather, salvation as available on condition of accepting "the word of reconciliation" (see 5:20: "we beg you on behalf of Christ, be reconciled to God"). Similarly, justification "for all people" in Romans 5:18 makes justification available for all, but not actual for all, because 2:2–6, 8–9 has previously spoken of suffering God's wrath at the Last Judgment. And again similarly, Jesus' drawing "all people" to himself according to John 12:32 cannot imply universal salvation; for 5:29 has referred to "the resurrection of judgment" as opposed to "the resurrection of life," and 3:36 has said that God's wrath "remains" on unbelievers, so that "all people" in 12:32 has to mean all kinds of people, such as non-Jews, "the Greeks" who had just asked to see Jesus (12:20–21; compare Revelation 5:9; 7:9). So talk of "tension" between supposedly universalistic texts and obviously nonuniversalistic texts amounts to a violation of the first rule of interpretation: Take account of the context.

The destruction of both soul and body in hell (Matthew 10:28) connotes devastation and ruination, not annihilation (compare the underlying Greek word's frequent use for lostness, as in the cases of the lost sheep, the lost coin, and the Prodigal Son, none of them annihilated [Luke 15:4, 6, 8–9, 24]). The doctrine of annihilation also runs into the difficulty that a shortening of punishment does not at all answer the question, Why does God not give everybody an equal opportunity to be saved? Besides, eternality characterizes future punishment to the same degree that it characterizes future bliss (note the parallelism in Matthew 25:46).

On to forms of so-called inclusivism, then. Usually hallowed with a supportive reference to the opinion of C. S. Lewis—though his associated belief in purgatory goes unmentioned—three inclusivistic answers to our question have captured more serious attention among conservative evangelicals. The first affirms the possibility of salvation through the revelation of God in the visible creation and in the human conscience. People who respond to this general revelation have the benefits of Jesus' redemptive work applied to them without their hearing and believing the gospel in this lifetime. The second answer affirms a hearing of the gospel upon death by all those who had not heard it before. Then they gain the opportunity of which they were deprived during their lifetimes. The third answer combines the first two: those who responded well to general revelation but did not hear the gospel—they but they alone will have an opportunity after dying. In view of their good response to general revelation, post-mortem belief in Christ will probably follow as a matter of course.

Proponents of these views make several appeals to Scripture. The Gentiles Melchizedek, Balaam, and Job (not to mention Adam, Abel, Seth, Enoch, and Noah, who lived prior to God's special revelation distinguishing Gentiles from Abraham and his offspring through Isaac and Jacob) are marched out as examples of salvation through general revelation. But the appeal to them overlooks the possibility that their knowledge of God derived from an original special revelation of himself to humanity, a revelation that started the practice of religion and was passed on to succeeding generations of the whole human race (see the old but still valuable book by Samuel M. Zwemer, *The Origin of Religion* [New York: Loizeaux, 1945] and the anthropological studies cited there of W. Schmidt). The missionary drive of the early church and, even earlier, the wholesale prophetic and other Jewish attacks on pagan religions imply that by the time of Jesus God's special revelation of himself at the dawn of human history had long since suffered dysfunctional corruption.

Matthew 25:31–46 indicates that all nations will receive judgment according to their exercising or failing to exercise charity toward the wretched of the earth, whom Jesus identifies as his own brothers, not according to their hearing and believing the gospel or failing to do so. Thus it is claimed. But this interpretation, which has proved irresistible to many a Christian humanitarian, stumbles against Jesus' own definition of his brothers as those who do the heavenly Father's will (Matthew 12:50) as revealed specifically in the teaching of Jesus (see Matthew 7:21 with 7:24–27; 28:20), and even more seriously stumbles against the parallelism with Matthew 10, where the persecuted little ones needing shelter, food, and drink are not the world's needy in general but Christian missionaries in particular (see especially verse 42)! When viewed in its Matthean context, in other words, the passage turns out to militate against the view for which it is cited; for "one of these littlest brothers of mine" (verse 40) is seen to be a messenger of the gospel.

John 1:9 says that the Word enlightens every human being. But the context deals with the incarnate ministry of Christ as providing light, and John later shows awareness that the disciples need to be *sent* in order for the saving effects of that light to be felt (John 20:21–23). Furthermore, the gaining of Christ's light links with believing in Christ (John 1:9–13; 3:16–21; 8:12–30). We do better to say that John jumps from the old creation at the beginning (1:1–3) to the new creation, dating from the incarnation (1:4–18), than to think that he writes concerning a preincarnate and continuing general ministry of the Word through the light of reason and conscience. Therefore John 1:9 means that Jesus the Word *as preached in the gospel* brings the light of salvation to everyone who hears and believes.

To appeal to God's acceptance of Cornelius, his household, and others like him (Acts 10:1–2, 34–35) is to forget that Luke and Peter are not talking about people deficient of special revelation, but about God-fearers, that is, about Gentiles who know and follow the special revelation of God in the Old Testament. Such Gentiles frequented the synagogues, where they regularly heard the Scriptures read. Furthermore, God sent Peter to preach the gospel to these people. Hence, they hardly support the possibility of salvation for the unevangelized.

According to Acts 18:9–10, the Lord said to Paul, "I have many people in this city [Corinth]." But in view of Acts 13:48b ("and as many as had been appointed to eternal life believed"), it is worse than gratuitous to take the Lord's statement as referring to ignorant but acceptable people rather than to those foreordained to salvation through hearing and believing the gospel in their present lifetime. And again, the very fact that God sent Paul to preach the gospel to these people in Corinth takes away support for theories of salvation through general revelation and post-mortem belief in Christ.

Yes, the heathen do—or at least did—understand general revelation (Romans 1:19–20), but the whole thrust of Romans 1:18–3:18, 23 is that they along with the Jews stand under God's wrath because of their sin. Paul brings up general revelation to show that humankind has rejected it. Therefore the passage poses a liability, not an asset, to the views under discussion. Romans 2:14–16, combined with verses 6–7, 10–11, 13, has been thought to describe the good works of the Law as performed by conscientious heathen and to ascribe to such heathen salvation. But more than once in the early chapters of Romans Paul sets out brief statements that he later interprets in detail (compare 1:8–15 with 15:14–33, and 1:16–17 with 3:21–4:25), and in 8:1–4 he indicates that only those who are in Christ by faith and consequently have the Holy Spirit can fulfill the righteous requirement of the Law. Therefore 2:14–16 refers to *Christian* Gentiles (see, for example, C. E. B. Cranfield, *A Critical and Exegetical Commentary on Romans* [ICC; Edinburgh: T. & T. Clark, 1975], 1:155–56).

Certainly Paul's quoting Psalm 19:4 ("Their voice has gone out into all the earth, and their words to the ends of the world") in Romans 10:18 provides no substantiation of the possibility of salvation through the general revelation enjoyed by unevangelized people. For although the psalmist has general revelation in mind, Paul reapplies the phraseology to "the gospel . . . the word of [= concerning] Christ" (verses 16–17). As is well-known, reapplications of Old Testament passages typify Paul's style (for another example nearby, see Romans 9:25–26, where the word of God through Hosea concerning the restoration of *Israel* shifts to God's acceptance of *Gentiles* who believe the gospel). Furthermore (though not essential to the argument), those who have heard (verse 18) are probably the Jews, so that now God is turning his attention to the Gentiles, who have not yet heard (verses 19–21 and the whole of Romans 9–11).

Even though we were to construe Christ's preaching to the spirits in prison (1 Peter 3:18–20) as an offer of salvation to deceased human beings, the problem of the ignorant heathen would still beg for solution. For the text limits the proclamation to the spirits active during the antediluvian generation of Noah and then confined to prison. Moreover, these spirits were "disobedient." They were not the open-hearted kind of heathen the possibility of whose salvation some current theologians are exploring. And disobedient to what? General revelation alone? Can we be sure that the special revelation of a destructive flood formed no part of Noah's preaching of righteousness (compare Genesis 6:9–22; Hebrews 11:7; 2 Peter 2:5)?

But, of course, 1 Peter 3:18–20 probably does not at all refer to an offer of salvation to deceased human beings. The context favors a proclamation of triumph over demonic powers. Just as Jesus gained such vindication before them, so also at the Last Day his persecuted followers will gain vindication in the presence of their persecutors. As usual, when lacking qualification to the contrary, the term "spirits" refers to spirits of an angelic or demonic kind, not to the spirits of disembodied human beings.

Differences of phraseology distance the preaching of the gospel to the dead (1 Peter 4:6) from Christ's proclamation to the once disobedient spirits in prison. This latter text specifies the gospel and deceased human beings. But who are these deceased people, and when did they hear the gospel preached to them? Apparently they are deceased Christians who heard and believed the gospel prior to suffering martyrdom. For Peter writes of their suffering in the flesh as Christ did, that is, to the point of death (verse 1; compare 3:17–18). The gospel was preached to the martyrs. This happened before their deaths, naturally; otherwise they would not have suffered martyrdom for the gospel. During the present interim between their martyrdom and resurrection they enjoy a disembodied life with God (compare 2 Corinthians 5:8; Philippians 1:23). Peter designs his comments to steel living Christians against the possibility of their own martyrdom. The passage does not afford good grounds, then, for conversion after death.

Those who see an out for the unevangelized do so out of concern to avoid impugning the justice of God and sacrificing his love. A laudable concern! But do the suggestions of salvation through general revelation and of conversion after death in fact do the apologetic job they are intended to do? No, they fail. We must ask whether the preaching of the gospel to people in their present lifetime gives them a better opportunity to be saved than they would have had apart from such preaching. If it does, God remains unfair and unloving to let some hear while some do not hear. For then a very large proportion of human beings will suffer eternal loss because he did not give them so good an opportunity as he gave to others.

On the other hand, if for the sake of equal treatment God does not allow the preaching of the gospel to enhance the opportunity to be saved, we have no reason to preach the gospel, at least not so far as the eternal destiny of people is concerned. In fact, on the principle that the servant who knows his master's will and disobeys will receive many lashes but the servant who does not know it will receive few (Luke 12:47–48), it would be better not to preach the gospel to anybody. None would suffer disadvantage, and—since we know by observation that where the gospel is preached the majority usually reject it—many would escape a worse punishment for sinning against greater light. Oddly, the merciful thing would be *not* to preach the gospel; and the suffering and martyrdom of witness-bearing Christians becomes a cruel mistake if the unreached can be saved equally well without hearing the gospel in this lifetime.

And what of the many who have heard the gospel in the present life, but only from those whose conduct does not recommend the message or only from those who in other ways have failed to make it clear and convincing? We might also wonder about people whose backgrounds make them less susceptible to evangelism. The list of inequalities could go on and on. If we demand equal treatment of those who have never heard, others cry out for equal treatment too. The attempts to justify God's ways in salvation cannot stop with the ignorant heathen. The facile solutions here criticized rest on a philosophical view of the problem that is too simplistic and restricted—and on a theological view of our ability to justify God's ways that is too inflated (compare Romans 11:33–36).

Given the complexities of the case, we might also doubt our ability to recognize perfect equality even though we saw it right before our eyes. Who knows? Maybe the inequalities are only apparent. But we can make no such claim, since appearances run to the contrary. It is enough to say that intellects properly chastened through recognition of their own limitations and of the complexities attending our question will hesitate to mount either an accusation against God or an apology for him. We can hardly improve on Paul's statement that the fate of the lost demonstrates the wrath and power of God just as the salvation of believers demonstrates his mercy (Romans 9:22–23). At this point it becomes evident whether our thinking centers on God—from whom and through whom and for whom are all things (Romans 11:36)—or whether anthropology has encroached on theology.

The Scriptures stand alone as our source of information concerning the status of the unevangelized. As we have seen, the notions of salvation through general revelation and of an opportunity after death find no solid footing in Scripture. More than that, Scripture indicates the hopelessness of people apart from hearing and believing the gospel now. In Adam all human beings stand under condemnation (Romans 5:12–21). They have rejected general revelation (Romans 1:18–32). God's wrath remains on them apart from belief in Jesus the Son (John 3:36). The present is the time for such belief: "Behold, *now* is 'the acceptable time'; behold, *now* is 'the day of salvation'" (2 Corinthians 6:2). Most clearly of all for our question, Paul puts all these pieces together in Romans 10:9–16 by writing in uninterrupted succession about the necessity to salvation of confessing Jesus as Lord and calling on his name, about the necessity of believing in Jesus for calling on him, about the necessity of hearing of him for believing in him, about the necessity of our preaching the gospel for people's hearing of him, and about the necessity of sending for preaching. "So faith comes from hearing, and hearing through the word of Christ" (Romans 10:17). We can hardly fail to notice Paul's focus on the specific message preached concerning the Lord Jesus Christ. And the repeated rhetorical questions, each beginning "How shall they . . . ?" show this way of salvation to be the only way. Without the human witness here and now, an essential link is broken; the chain of salvation will not hold.

Since Scripture makes the unevangelized lost and our preaching the gospel to them necessary to their salvation, those who propose contrary views ought to adduce more cogent biblical evidence in favor of those views. Otherwise, we should have to move to a decanonized view of revelation as an ever-ongoing process. Biblical particularism and evangelistic necessity, which may have been good enough for olden times, could give way to post-biblical revelation of a theodicy supposedly more just and gracious and conveniently easier to swallow.

But the new truths of salvation by general revelation and of post-mortem conversion would doubtless yield to the even "better" truth of universal salvation. For someone is bound to ask why God even bothers to create beings who he knows ahead of time will respond neither to general revelation nor to special revelation, and why he allows many of them to increase their damnation by giving them more and more revelation that he knows very well they are not going to accept. Either we settle for a technically fair God (he gives everybody an equal opportunity) notably lacking in kindness (he creates people who he foresees will not take advantage of their equal opportunities). Or we save his kindness with the excuse of ignorance (he did not know that many of his creatures would destroy themselves, and even yet he mindlessly keeps on willing them into existence). Or, ironically, having rejected the Calvinistic doctrine of particular election we universalize the Calvinistic doctrine of irresistible grace. By this time we have strayed so far from Scripture that the whole problem, having lost its biosphere, ceases to exist.

Staying within Scripture, however, we discover behind the Great Commission a reason to evangelize the heathen more compelling than the desirability of bringing them into the joy of salvation a little earlier than otherwise they would enter it. The reason is that apart from our preaching to them the word of Christ, they have no hope. So let us urgently and compassionately rescue the perishing.

An Extended Note on Eternal Punishment

The New Testament doesn't put forward eternal punishment of the wicked as a doctrine to be defended because it casts suspicion on God's justice and love. To the contrary, the New Testament puts forward eternal punishment as right, even obviously right. It wouldn't be right of God not to punish the wicked, so that the doctrine supports rather than subverts his justice and love. It shows that he keeps faith with the righteous, that he loves them enough to vindicate them, that he rules according to moral and religious standards that really count, that moral and religious behavior has consequences, that wickedness gets punished as well as righteousness rewarded, and that the eternality of punishment as well as of reward invests the moral and religious behavior of human beings with ultimate significance. We're not playing games. In short, the doctrine of eternal punishment defends God's justice and love and supplies an answer to the problem of moral and religious evil rather than contributing to the problem.

God will finally rectify all the imbalances in the scales of justice. To biblical people no mystery attached to this rectification, as though to say we can't understand it now—how it could be right for God to punish the wicked eternally—but at the Last Day we'll recognize his love and justice in punishing them eternally and rewarding the righteous, also eternally. To biblical people it was *already* clear that by so doing, God will be exercising his love and justice. And it was already clear to them because they had an acute, firsthand awareness of the depth of human depravity, on the one hand, and of the pain of man's inhumanity to man, on the other hand.

Often, moderns think that if only biblical people hadn't been so insular, if only they'd lived in the times of radio, television, the internet, international travel, if only they'd been personally acquainted with people of other religions—some Buddhists, Hindus, Muslims—they wouldn't have come up with the horrible idea of eternal punishment. But the doctrine of divine inspiration of Scripture aside (though it warrants acceptance), biblical people were probably less insular than we moderns are. Most of them had closer and more numerous contacts with people of other religions then we do. As to most of the people we Christians in the western world deal with, if they aren't Christians they've at least been deeply influenced by the side-effects of the Christian faith that have permeated our culture. But biblical people rubbed shoulders daily with those who diligently practiced other religions, usually a variety of other religions at the same time. They knew what those other religions were and what effects they had on people. So maybe the problem we modern westerners feel in regard to the doctrine of eternal punishment arises out of *our* comparative insularity, not out of the insularity of those who wrote the Bible, to *our* relative ignorance of the realities of human nature, other religions, and their effects on human behavior. At any rate, it's simply wrong to attribute the doctrine to unfamiliarity with other religions and their devotees.

To reference the righteous and the wicked in this discussion isn't to imply that people gain eternal life or suffer eternal punishment on the basis of whether their conduct is, on the whole, good or bad. Thinking that they do is probably part of the problem modern westerners have in accepting the Bible's teaching of eternal punishment: Non-Christians often seem to be good people. Why should they be punished forever? But people's conduct isn't necessarily an accurate gauge of whether their *nature* is good or bad. Relatively good conduct can be the accidental effect of a good environment in family, friends, teachers, and the surrounding general culture. Put supposedly good people in another set of circumstances—a set in which they can do what they jolly well please, for example, or in which they're subject to greater temptation—and they may turn into Hitlers. Take Nero. At first, when still under the influence of the Stoic philosopher Seneca, Nero was a fairly good Roman emperor. After Seneca died, though, Nero turned demonic. We just don't know people's hearts, or even our own hearts, as God knows them (Jeremiah 17:9–10). People don't go to heaven because their conduct is good enough. They don't go to hell because their conduct is too bad, but because they themselves are bad whether or not that fact has come out very clearly in their conduct. Our conduct and our eternal fate aren't related directly to each other as cause and effect. They're both the effect of whether or not we've been born from above through faith in Jesus Christ and the action of God's Spirit. What our conduct does determine, however, is the degree to which we enjoy eternal life or suffer eternal punishment (see, for example, Luke 12:47–48; 1 Corinthians 3:10–15). Though *purely* enjoyable, heaven won't be *equally* enjoyable for everybody there. Similarly, hell won't be equally torturous for everybody there, and not so torturous as to impugn God's justice—yet torturous enough to be avoided at all costs.

Part Four:

Valedictory Talks

Soli Deo Gloria

~ Delivered at a baccalaureate service ~

My colleagues on the faculty and staff of Westmont, trustees of the college, families and friends of our graduating seniors, and, above all, you graduating seniors yourselves, in the beginning was the word. I don't mean Jesus the Word. I mean the word "commencement." Originally, it meant "beginning." It still does outside schools and colleges at springtime.

But the word has changed its meaning. Here on campus, this evening, it means just the opposite of a beginning. It means an ending, the ending of a college career. Oh, I know, we've all heard speeches proclaiming that commencement isn't the end of your education; it's just a beginning, the beginning of a lifelong education, the first day of the rest of your educational life. Maybe so; we certainly hope so. But the stubborn fact remains that in current usage—and if modern linguistics has taught us anything, it has taught us that words mean what they mean *now*, in their present context, not what they *used* to mean—the stubborn fact remains that in current usage at this time and in this place, "commencement" means the end of a college career. A successful end, to be sure; but definitely an end.

Ah, but this isn't commencement, you say; it's baccalaureate. Commencement doesn't come till tomorrow. You're right, of course; but the word "baccalaureate" has changed too. "Baccalaureate" is just a different way of saying "bachelaureate." It used to mean honoring students—that is to say, bachelors, because married men had pursuits other than scholarship, which comes from a Greek word meaning "leisure," such as only bachelors have; and not even single women had the chance for scholarship they should have had. "Baccalaureate" meant honoring bachelors (that's the "bacca"-part of "bacca-laureate") with the laurel wreath of an academic degree (that's the "laureate"-part). "Baccalaureate": honoring students with a bachelor's degree.

But when do we honor students with a bachelor's degree? Not at baccalaureate, but at commencement! "Bacca-laureate" has *come* to mean the honoring, not of successful students, but of God. So let's be clear what we're doing here. We're not honoring you students. We're not honoring your families and friends. We're not honoring teachers, staff, trustees, or other people who may have helped you toward your degree. We are honoring God, and God alone.

This is a service of worship, then, for you graduating seniors your final service of worship as a student at this college. The theme for the service comes from Dietrich Bonhoeffer: "The more exclusively we acknowledge and confess Christ as our Lord, the more fully the wide range of His dominion will be disclosed to us." The title for this message, "Soli Deo Gloria," meaning "To God Alone Be the Glory," comes from Johann Sebastian Bach, who attached this phrase to his musical scores. Our scriptural text comes from St. Paul's Epistle to the Philippians 2:1–11:

> So if in Christ you have any encouragement to give me, any loving comfort, any sharing of the Spirit, any affection and compassion, make me happy by adopting the same attitude, which means loving each other the same, developing mutual affection toward each other, adopting this attitude alone, not doing anything by way of self-assertion or with a sense of superiority, which in any case is mistaken, but with a lowly attitude regarding each other as

superior to yourselves, not looking out just for your own interests, but each person also for the interests of others. Adopt among yourselves this attitude so as to prove that you too are in Christ Jesus, who, though existing in the form of God, did not treat his being equal with God as something to be taken advantage of, but emptied himself by taking the form of a slave, having already come to be in the likeness of human beings. And already found to have the identity of a human being, he lowered himself by becoming obedient to the extent of death, even death on a cross. Therefore also God has lifted him above everyone else and given him the name above every other name, in order that at the name which Jesus has every knee should bow of heavenly and earthly and underworldly beings—and every tongue should confess, "Jesus Christ is Lord," to the glory of God the Father.

This passage says three things about Christian people: First, their discipleship entails community with other believers in Jesus. Second, their community with those other believers requires humility toward them. Third and above all, their humility models the humility of Jesus himself.

Years ago *The Manchester Guardian* (nowadays just *The Guardian*) advertised itself as the newspaper for people who think. Not to be outdone, *The Glasgow Herald* advertised itself as the newspaper for people who think for themselves. Graduating seniors, you've received a higher education. That kind of education breeds a certain independence of mind. You've become Glaswegans. You've learned to think for yourselves. You make your own judgments, your own decisions, your own choices. You not only believe *what* you believe; you know *why* you do. You understand, you even appreciate, arguments for contrary beliefs. But when you reject those arguments, you reject them intelligently, not pigheadedly. So far so good.

As with all good things, however, there's a danger; and here it is: independence of thought can easily lead to isolation and skepticism. Allow the reduction of yourself to that famous Cartesian starting point, "I think; therefore I am," and you'll live alone with your thoughts, increasingly skeptical and increasingly alone, wrongly skeptical and wrongly alone. But a really good higher education, particularly a Christian one, teaches you to think not only for yourself, but also in community with other people, especially in community with other Christians.

You've inherited a tradition, Christianity, which in our case includes a Christian version of the liberal arts and sciences. We believe that Christianity is true; but it's still traditional, because "traditional" means "handed on," as Christianity is, from one person and generation to another. The very idea of tradition includes community. Some of us have passed our tradition on to you. Now you're going to bear that tradition, add to it your own contributions, and then pass it on to others. "No man is an island, entire of itself" (John Donne). None of us live to ourselves; we live in relation to the Lord and the people around us. So Christian discipleship entails community. It did at the start. When the twelve apostles followed Jesus about Palestine, they formed a community around his person. Then they formed a larger community in Jerusalem. And so on. Christian discipleship continues to entail community: wherever they live, believers in Jesus form communities around his name.

The apostle Paul writes his prison epistle called Philippians to just such a community, one that's distant from him. He appeals to them: Make me happy! I'm in prison. Encourage me. Do you love me enough to comfort me? Do you feel sorry for me at all? Then let me hear that you're living together in community. "If in Christ you have any encouragement to give me," Paul writes, "prove that you, too, are in Christ." All of us believers are in Christ. It's not just our faith that's in him. By faith *we* are in him. And if we're there, in him, we can't help but come close together. No Christian community, no position in Christ. You show the one by the other.

Your present Christian community is one day away from breaking up, graduating seniors. A few of us will be staying here, but most of you will be scattering to distant parts, scattering from us who stay and scattering from one another. Some of you can hardly wait to leave. Others of you may be shedding a tear or two. But in either case, or if you have mixed feelings, wherever you go, establish community with others of like faith. In those distant places, make us who stay "imprisoned" here at Westmont—make us happy by living and thinking and feeling in cohesion with fellow believers. Let us hear that you are proving the genuineness of your Christian discipleship, that you are people of community, church-people, traditioners, not loners.

Second, Christian community requires humility, and humility means lowliness. A higher education doesn't always produce lowliness. The very word "higher" tempts us to be uppity. But a Christian higher education should belie the higher part of its name and produce lowliness. It takes lowliness to love each other the same. It takes lowliness to develop mutual affection toward each other. It takes lowliness to consider others superior to yourself rather than yourself superior to them. It takes lowliness to look after their interests as much as your own.

The world tells you, "Feel good about yourself, build yourself up." Jesus tells you, "Repent of your sins." The world tells you, "Assert yourself." Jesus tells you, "Deny yourself." The world tells you, "Love yourself." Jesus tells you, "Love God, and love your neighbor as you love yourself without having to be told to." Don't imitate those victorious Olympians interviewed on television after winning a gold or silver or bronze: "I'm proud of what I did today. I worked hard for this medal. I deserved it." Don't strut and swagger. Wear your bachelor's degree with grace and humility. Think of it as a means of serving others better, not as a means of bettering yourself.

And resist credentialism. Don't sign your letters "John Doe, BA" or "Jane Doe, MA, PhD" if you go on to advanced degrees. Your name is good enough by itself. People won't care about your degrees anyway. Nor should they. They'll care about your character and deeds. So will God. Your degree is only as good as it broadens and deepens your God-like humanity by refining your character, expanding your knowledge, and sharpening your wisdom, so that you turn into a better servant of God and of the gospel of his Son Jesus Christ, into a better servant of the church and of the world at large.

You may think I'm trying to rain on this academic parade by degrading your degree. Not in the least. Celebrate. By all means celebrate. Party. Have a good time. But celebrate in a spirit of humble thanksgiving, not in a spirit of boastful pride. As Paul says, regard others as better than yourselves. It helps us regard others as better than ourselves to remember that they might very well *be* better

than we are, whatever our academic or other credentials—
or theirs. Give credit to others. Let others give credit to
you. And let us all give credit, indeed all ultimate credit, to
God, the giver of every good and perfect gift that makes
possible celebrations like this one.

Third and above all, Christian humility models the
humility of Jesus himself. An attitude of humility among
us equates with the same attitude on his part. "Adopt
among yourselves this attitude, proving that you too are in
Christ Jesus." With this command Paul launches into his
famous, fullscale description of Jesus' humility: its background, its outworking, and its rewards.

The description begins with the background of Jesus'
preexistence and ends with his postexistence, the before
and after of his earthly career. As the text says,
preexistence in the form of God means such a close
correspondence to God that it's no exaggeration to speak
of equality with God. So preexistence means divine
existence.

Jesus' postexistence divides into past and future. God has
already performed a double action on him: first, he has
lifted Jesus above everyone else; second, he has given him
a name above every other name—a kind of supreme
baccalaureate. These two actions, in turn, have a double
purpose yet to be fulfilled: first, that every knee should
bow at the name given to Jesus; second, that every tongue
should confess that that name does indeed belong to him.

And what is the name? It's the name "Lord." "Jesus Christ
is Lord." In Hebrew, Yahweh, "LORD" all capital letters
in English. In the Greek that Paul used, it's *kyrios,* which
means "sir, master, owner, emperor, deity, Lord" all in one
breath. The most holy of divine names, the most revered,
the most sacred—so sacred that Jewish scribes used an

antique style of writing, something like Gothic script, when copying the name, so revered that at first they didn't translate it even when they were translating all the surrounding text. There can be no name higher than this one. Here's the name that God has given to Jesus, then, the name at the mention of which on the Last Day every knee will bow, the name that every tongue will pronounce as indicating the true and honored identity of Jesus Christ.

So Paul begins and ends on high notes: Jesus' preexistence meant divine existence. His postexistence has brought him divine honors, and will yet bring him divine honors. But in the middle, Paul strikes some low notes. This divine equal of God put on human dress. He came to be like us, not like us as nearly human, but like us as truly and fully human. He looked like us because he was one of us. People found him to be human because he was human.

> That glorious form, that light unsufferable,
> And that far-beaming blaze of majesty
> Wherewith he wont at Heaven's high council-table
> To sit the midst of Trinal Unity,
> He laid aside; and here with us to be,
> Forsook the courts of everlasting day,
> And chose with us a darksome house of mortal clay.
> (John Milton)

> Out of the bosome of eternall blisse,
> In which he reigned with his glorious Syre,
> He downe descended, like a most demisse
> And abject thrall, in fleshes fraile attyre,
> That he for him might pay sinnes deadly hyre . . . .
> In flesh at first the guilt committed was,
> Therefore in flesh it must be satisfyde . . . .

> So, taking flesh of sacred virgins wombe
> For mans deare sake he did a man become.
>
> (Edmund Spenser)

Deity—humanity. Heaven—Bethlehem. Preexistence—birth. You might think these are the contrasts Paul has in mind. But no, the one who existed in the form of God as God's equal, the one who has already received divine honors from God and will yet receive them from all God's creatures—he didn't become a human being just for a cross-cultural experience. Oh no! He became a human being to qualify himself for a cross. The real contrasts don't lie between deity and humanity, heaven and Bethlehem, preexistence and birth. The real contrasts lie between deity and slavery, between heaven and Golgotha, between preexistence and death.

"He emptied himself" doesn't mean that Jesus emptied himself of his deity by taking on humanity. The statement doesn't refer to the incarnation at all, but to what the incarnation made possible. "He emptied himself" means exactly what Isaiah 53:12 says about the Suffering Servant of the Lord: "he poured out his soul to death." "Poured out," "emptied"—they're synonymous. "Soul," "life," "self"—they're all the same, as when Jesus said that he came to give his life (it's the same as the word for "soul") —he came to give his life, his soul, as a ransom for many; and Paul echoes those words in 1 Timothy 2:5–6: "the man Christ Jesus . . . gave himself as a ransom." Notice how "self" substitutes for "soul" or "life." Isaiah says that the Servant of the Lord poured out his soul, his life, himself to the extent of death; and Paul says that as a servant, a slave, Jesus became obedient to the extent of death.

Not at his birth, then, but at the cross Jesus emptied himself by taking the form of a servant, a slave; for he died the death of a cross, the punishment of a slave. That's what the Romans called crucifixion: "a slave's punishment." They used it especially for slaves to keep them from rebelling. Others, too, might suffer crucifixion; but if they did, they were being treated as slaves. Cicero called it the most cruel and disgusting penalty. According to him "the very word 'cross' should be far removed not only from the person of a Roman citizen, but from his thoughts, his eyes, and his ears. For it is not only the actual occurrence . . . or the endurance . . . but . . . the very mention [of crucifixion] . . . that is unworthy of a Roman citizen and a free man."

It was a cruel death, as the senator said; but that's not Paul's point. It was—and here Paul agrees with Cicero—it was a disgusting death, a shameful one. Stripped of clothing. Nakedness exposed to public view. Not even a loincloth (despite the modesty in Christian art). Taunted and jeered by onlookers. No death with dignity here—only shame and utter degradation.

So the ancient formula of crucifixion went like this: "Go tie up his hands. Cover his head. Hang him on the tree of shame." And the Latin author Juvenal wrote up this conversation between a Roman matron and her husband: "'Crucify that slave,' says the wife. 'But what crime worthy of death has he committed?' asks the husband. . . . 'At least give him a hearing. No delay can be too long when the life of a human being is at stake!' 'What a numskull you are! [answers the wife]. Do you call a slave a human being?'" To be crucified was to be treated as subhuman.

Jesus emptied himself. He lowered himself. So low, so shameful his death that Paul writes, "even death on a cross." Actually, the word he uses for "even" has a stronger meaning: "but." Jesus lowered himself by becoming obedient to the extent of death—but death on a cross, as though death on a cross is so shameful that it stands by itself, over against every other kind of death. And not *the* cross, shining symbol of the Christian religion, set on church steeples and spires and domes of cathedrals, or an article of jewelry made of gold or silver. No, not that cross. Just *a* cross: "but death on a cross." It could have been any cross, an ordinary piece of wood used to inflict extraordinary shame, the shame of a slave's punishment.

Now death by a slave's punishment suits the role of Jesus as a slave. But he's the Slave, the Servant, of the Lord; so when Paul says that Jesus was "obedient to death," he doesn't mean that death was giving the orders, as when in literature and film—Bergman's "Seventh Seal," for example—the angel of death knocks at the door, says "Come," and there's no resisting, because you have to go; you have to die. "Obedient to death" refers to the freely given obedience of God's equal to the will of God that he, Jesus Christ, go to the extent of dying the punishment of a slave to redeem those enslaved by sin and death. In the very nature of the case, there can be no obedience greater than sacrificing your life. Once you've rendered that obedience, you can do no more. You're dead. Just so with the obedience of Jesus. It went, as we say, to the max.

But I've cheated: I've told you the purpose of Jesus' obedience: our redemption. The apostle Paul skips over that purpose entirely. At this point he isn't interested in *why* Jesus died, only in *how* he died. Attention concentrates solely on the shame of his death, so that we may see more clearly in all its startling grandeur God's exaltation of Jesus, an exaltation that more than compensates for his humiliation. Out of the depths of that humiliation arises the height of his exaltation: "therefore also God has lifted him above everyone else and given him the name above every other name." Highest honor has replaced deepest shame. Summa cum laude! Par excellence!

And further honors will come. At the Last Day, when our tale has been told and the smoke of burning civilizations, having thrown themselves into the cauldron of their own lusts for power, privilege, and pleasure—when their smoke darkens the sun and reddens the moon, as Scripture says, when falling stars rain down in a storm whose lightning consists of streaking meteorites, whose thunder comes from the sound of their impact, when the earth heaves and groans, cracks and shudders in a last great earthquake, the mother of all big ones, when volcanoes explode, spewing out rivers of fire and brimstone, in that final convulsion of fallen history, the dreadful intersection of geology, astronomy, human decadence, and divine retribution, the heavens will part and Jesus Christ will appear robed in glory, radiant in splendor, crowned with majesty, dominion, and power. At the sight of him, kings and queens will descend their thrones, dictators and presidents and athletes their pedestals, and stars of stage and screen, conductors, performers, all the idolized and lionized, politicians and CEOs and scholars and teachers, BAs, MAs, MBAs, PhDs, MDs, rich and poor and middle class, angels and demons, cherubim and seraphim, Gabriel, Michael, yes, the Devil himself—all, without exception, all God's creatures, all of us will fall on our knees, momentarily stupefied at the sight of Jesus.

Then body-language will yield to words, and in a mighty chorus, resounding from highest heaven and lowest hell and from the farthest reaches of earth, the all who have bowed their knees will recover their senses and their voices and join together in a grand verbal ovation, "Jesus Christ is Lord!" For dramatic emphasis, Paul's original text has no verb "is," and puts the name "Lord" first: "Lord—Jesus Christ!" No one will fail to recognize the true identity of Jesus or refuse to acknowledge the universal extent of his authority. From slavish obedience to imperial mastery! But before the last echo of our thunderous acclamation of Jesus' lordship has trailed off to the edge of space, I suspect we shall hear a lone voice answering back. It will be the voice of Jesus himself, his hand upraised, not in blessing, but with finger pointing heavenward, and in tones whose echo will never fall silent, but reverberate throughout eternity, world without end. He will say, "To the glory of God the Father." Even then, still then, when we've all confessed his lordship, when he stands universally acclaimed as supreme over all creatures, great and small, he will be, and will ever be, the one who does not treat equality with God as something to be taken advantage of.

Well now, your bachelor's degree won't come up to the level of equality with God. But it is something— something quite considerable, in fact. How will you treat it? Soli Deo Gloria.

Run for Your Life

~ Delivered at another baccalaureate service ~

Mr. President, trustees, colleagues on the faculty, friends and guests, but above all, and most affectionately, members of the graduating class, at first it seemed like a high honor that I'd be asked to give this baccalaureate address. But then a note came telling me the topic I was supposed to speak on and the passage of Scripture that was supposed to be my text: Philippians 3:4b–14. Suddenly everything became clear. You students were getting back at me for all the assignments I'd given you by giving *me* an assignment, rather like the game of "last touch." Well, as children we used to say, "Turn about's fair play." Now that we're educated we say, "Poetic justice"; but it means the same thing.

> If anyone else thinks he has reason to put confidence in the flesh, I have more: circumcised on the eighth day, of the nation of Israel, of the tribe of Benjamin, a Hebrew of Hebrews; as to the Law, a Pharisee; as to zeal, a persecutor of the church; as to the righteousness that's in the Law, blameless. But whatever things were gain to me, those things I counted as loss for the sake of Christ. Yes, truly, and I am counting all things as loss because of the surpassing value of knowing Christ Jesus my Lord, for whom I've suffered the loss of all things, and I'm counting them as dung in order that I may gain Christ and be found in him, not having a righteousness of my own derived from the Law but having that which is through faith in Christ, the righteousness which comes from God on the basis of faith, that I may know him and the power of his resurrection and the fellowship of his sufferings, being conformed to his death; in order

> that I may attain the resurrection from the dead.
> Not that I have already obtained it or have already
> become perfect, but I press on that I may lay hold
> of that for which also I was laid hold of by Christ
> Jesus. Brothers and sisters, I do not regard myself
> as having yet laid hold of it; but one thing I do:
> forgetting the things behind and reaching forward
> to the things ahead, I'm pressing on toward the goal
> for the prize of the upward call of God in Christ
> Jesus.

What a passage of Scripture to be assigned! The question
is whether we can do it justice—any kind of justice:
poetic, theological, exegetical, or what-have-you. Reading
this passage usually makes our minds center on the marvel
of Paul's conversion. A classic conversion it was! *The*
classic conversion. Think of it: Paul was a blue-blooded
Jew, a rabbinical student, a Pharisee so zealous for his
religion that he was persecuting Christians. He had already
moved up through the ranks—the valedictorian of the
class of A.D. 34 in the School of Gamaliel. The career
scouts couldn't wait to interview him and offer him
contracts. Then in one swift motion the long arm of the
exalted Christ reached down, nabbed Paul by the nape of
his neck, shook him till his Pharisaic teeth rattled out,
dropped him to the ground, picked him up again, and
propelled him out into the world—now as a proclaimer of
Christ instead of a persecutor of Christians. This was no
half-baked conversion. If Jesus called disciples to become
fishers of men, Paul was the Compleat Angler.

Listen to our passage, though. Its main thrust has to do
with the *in*completeness of Paul's conversion: "*Not* that I
have already obtained it [the resurrection] or have already
become perfect . . . . I do *not* regard myself as having yet

laid hold of it." Translated for you: You're not done yet. The diploma is not in hand. It's not time to switch your tassel. Faith in Christ isn't only for conversion. It's for your whole Christian life, from start to finish. In fact, conversion itself isn't just something that happened; it keeps on happening. If it was a true conversion, it's not only permanent. It's progressive. "Whatever things were gain to me, those I *counted* as loss for the sake of Christ" —past tense. "Yes, truly, and I *am* counting all things as loss"—present tense.

There's not only chronological progress. There's also widening scope: "Whatever things were *gain* to me, those things I counted as loss." "I am counting *all* things as loss." No funny money rolling off the presses to paper over the difference between red ink and black ink here. No, sir. Plus against minus. Profit against loss. Assets against deficits. Christ against the self-made man.

Furthermore, there's increasing intensity. "I am counting them as *loss*" changes to "I'm counting them as *dung.*" A book-keeping metaphor turns into the figure of feces. The language isn't refined. It's gross, in fact. Maturity doesn't mellow Paul. It makes him more radical than ever.

Now ask yourself seriously whether you, like Paul, continue to disregard the things you gave up to follow Christ. Or are they creeping back into your life, especially now that you seem well-furnished with a college education to make a success of yourself in the world? Ask yourself seriously whether you disregard more and more things in order to follow Christ. Or has the list stayed pretty much the same for a long time, or perhaps become shorter? And ask yourself seriously whether your opinion of worldly success is getting worse, so that it means less and less to you whether you get ahead in the world.

You'll notice that Paul makes this kind of growing detachment from worldly success a condition: a condition for *knowing* Christ, a condition for *gaining* Christ, a condition for being *found* in Christ, a condition even for attaining the *resurrection from the dead*. Paul means the resurrection to salvation, of course. In other words, you're not saved yet—not completely. Sure, you may have grown up in a Christian atmosphere, put your faith in Christ, gone on Potter's Clay, and won some people to Christ. Praise God for all that has happened to you and through you by God's grace. But Paul experienced a lot more than you've ever experienced, and did a lot more than you've ever done. Yet he still talked about *attaining* the resurrection. In one passage he even said that he beat his body black and blue and made it his slave—a vivid figure for his self-denying life-style—lest possibly after preaching to others he himself should be disqualified (1 Corinthians 9:27; compare 2 Corinthians 13:5). It's not a question of being a good Christian or a bad one, then. It's a question of being a Christian or not. Salvation itself is at stake.

So ask yourself those questions again, and be more serious about them this time. You have everything to gain and everything to lose: time and eternity, heaven and hell, this life and the next. What will it be? It hinges—it all hinges—on whether you increasingly reject worldly gain in order to gain Christ, or whether your ardor to know Christ cools off because you increasingly try to advance yourself.

Do you hear, really hear, what Paul is saying? He's saying that what you do with your college education will show whether your professed Christian faith is genuine or not and therefore whether you'll participate in the resurrection to eternal life. Admittedly, this isn't the kind of talk a person expects to hear on a festive occasion like the one we're celebrating this evening. Congratulations are in better order. But I can't help it what the Holy Spirit inspired Paul to write, nor can I help it that that same Spirit guided you to assign me this passage. Who wants to evade the truth anyway, especially when you've spent four years and a lot of money looking for it?

Paul's original assets consisted in status, which he inherited, and achievements, which he racked up. Both were Jewish, and he depended on both. Your assets are almost certainly different, maybe birth into a wealthy home with all the material and educational and cultural advantages that brings. Or maybe it's growing up in a warm, lively, evangelistic church that gave you a head start. Now you add to such inherited blessings a Christian liberal arts education. Appreciate these blessings, but don't depend on them. In comparison with depending on Christ and on him alone, Paul says to despise all such assets as being liabilities. Your advantages of birth and upbringing, your education, your religious accomplishments—none of them cut any ice with God. The only thing that does—the *only* thing that does—is knowing Christ. Not just knowing him in conversion, though that's included—and necessary, so necessary, in fact, that I'm led to ask whether it's possible, whether it's true, that you're graduating without ever having come to know Christ, even for the first time, despite chapels and courses in Bible and theology, despite Christian teachers, Christian counselors, and fellow-students who are Christians. Say it isn't so. But if it is, you haven't graduated quite yet and I give you a last appeal: Get acquainted with Christ now. It's not too late.

I'm speaking to parents, other loved ones, and guests as well. The good news concerning salvation in Christ is for you too. Your sons and daughters, brothers and sisters and friends who are graduating may know someone you don't know, but whom to know brings life eternal. They join me in inviting you to accept this introduction to Jesus as your Lord and Savior, the one who died for your sins, rose from the dead, and will come back to judge the whole human race. Meet him now—the right way, the beneficial way—by repentance and faith. We'd have more cause than ever to celebrate if you were to do that. A Christian baptism is better than a college diploma any day.

But knowing Christ goes on and on and on after you've met him. What does it mean to keep on knowing him, and how can you as a Christian believer know Christ, gain Christ, be found in him, and attain the resurrection? Paul doesn't leave us guessing. He defines knowing Christ first as knowing the power of his resurrection, second as knowing the fellowship of his sufferings, and third as being conformed to his death. Let's take these in order.

First, to know the power of Christ's resurrection is to experience at work in your own life the same power of God the Father that raised Christ from the dead—at work in your own life now, in advance of the resurrection, so that when your resurrection does take place, it won't be an interruption. It will be the finishing touch, the proofreading of the term paper that God is already writing on your life (so far in rough draft). "Therefore, we have been buried with him through baptism into death in order that as Christ was raised from the dead through the glory of the Father, so we too might walk in newness of life. . . . alive to God in Christ Jesus. . . . alive from the dead . . . instruments of righteousness to God" (Romans 6:4, 11, 13).

Second, to know the fellowship of Christ's sufferings is to suffer to make the gospel *known* in the world just as Christ suffered that there might *be* a gospel. Listen to Paul's words from Romans 8 and Colossians 1: "Tribulation, distress, persecution, famine, nakedness, peril, sword. As it's written, 'For your sake we are being put to death all day long. We are considered as sheep to be slaughtered.'" We are "filling up what is lacking in the afflictions of Christ." People won't be saved if we don't sacrifice to the point of suffering so that they may hear the gospel, anymore than they'd be saved if Christ hadn't died and risen in the first place. You'll notice that Paul puts knowing the power of Christ's resurrection ahead of the fellowship of his sufferings even though things happened the other way around for Christ (Good Friday before Easter). And Paul clamps together the power of Christ's resurrection and fellowship of his sufferings in the tightest possible way, because we wouldn't be able to suffer with Christ without having God's almighty power to sustain us—the very power that snapped the cords of death for Christ. But knowing the surpassing greatness of this power, as Paul says in 2 Corinthians 4:8–12, "We're afflicted in every way but not crushed, perplexed but not despairing, persecuted but not forsaken, struck down but not destroyed, always carrying about in the body the dying of Jesus that also the life of Jesus may be manifested in our body. For we who live are constantly being delivered over to death for Jesus' sake that also the life of Jesus may be manifested in our mortal flesh. So death works in us, but life in you."

Third, to be conformed to Christ's death is to say with Paul, "God forbid that I should boast except in the cross of our Lord Jesus Christ, through which the world has been crucified to me and I to the world" (Galatians 6:14). It's to consider ourselves dead to sin. It's refusing—in the potent name of Christ and from the point of view which God

221

takes concerning us, that we died to sin when Christ died—refusing to let sin reign so as to obey its lusts.

Now all these phrases make high-sounding theological jargon, you're saying, but let's be practical. How does a person, a Christian person, get to the point of knowing Christ according to these definitions? Paul has anticipated your question and describes certain ways and means of experiencing the power of Christ's resurrection, the fellowship of his sufferings, and conformity to his death. The first is to forget the things behind you. "The things behind" are your inherited status and your achievements up to this point. Forget them. Go on to something more, something better. Don't hang around us like grownup children who don't know it's time to leave home. We like you, we love you, too much to want you here anymore. You're educated for the world, not to be coddled and cuddled forever in the womb of our college. Four years' gestation is long enough for any human being. So get going. Forget us. You have more important things to do, things for God and his kingdom. "Forget" doesn't mean "blot out from your memory," as though you *could* forget in that sense (and as though the Alumni Office won't keep reminding you where you've been). It means not to let your inherited status and past achievements lock up your God-given possibilities for the future. The Lord has much more for you than he has shown you thus far.

Second, put your whole self into the Christian life. Reach for it. Go for it. Don't lounge backwards into the kingdom as though it were an easy chair. This is a race. Run forward. Keep your eyes ahead. Stretch. Like a sprinter, strain for the tape. Let every muscle be taut, every vein bulge out. You're not jogging for your health; you're running for your life—your eternal life.

Third, always keep the goal in sight. Never let temptation, the desire to break loose and take a breather, and never let self-ambition throw you off track. In a physical education course I once had, the coach took the class to one end of a football field. Then he divided the class in half and told the first half to run to the other end. I was in the second half. While the other students were running down the field, the coach said to the rest of us, "Watch them. See how they're weaving back and forth." Sure enough, they were reeling their way downfield like drunks. They must have run 110 yards instead of 100. Then the coach called them back and said, "I want you to run the length of the field again. But this time pick an object straight in front of you, and run for it. Don't take your eyes off it." (The coach was a crusty old soul; he didn't believe in modern nonsense about non-Euclidean geometry; so far as he was concerned the shortest distance between two points is still a straight line.) The students ran again, and this time they ran straight. You could see the difference. They ran only the distance they had to—no wasted energy, no wasted time. That's the only way to win the prize.

But even though you do win the prize that way, it's God's call, not your effort, that's the sole source of your salvation. God's call means the special work of grace by which he saves you and sanctifies you and ultimately glorifies you. It stresses that your effort is not something you can take pride in, or credit for, even though your effort is a necessary indication that God really has called you. All the credit goes to Jesus. For God's call, Paul says, is in Christ Jesus—in him who died for us and rose and ascended to God's right hand in heaven. And in union with Christ we died, we rose, and we ascended. When we run the Christian race, we're simply catching up to what has already happened to us in Christ.

Paul adds that God's call in Christ Jesus is an upward call. Some people think that means being called up to heaven when we die, or when Jesus comes back at the end of the race. But Paul explains himself differently in his letter to the Colossians. "If then you've been raised up with Christ, keep seeking the things above, where Christ is seated at the right hand of God. Set your mind on the things above, not on the things that are on earth. For you've died, and your life is hidden with Christ in God" (Colossians 3:1–3). That much sounds like what I've said some people think. But what are the things above, the "upward things"? (It's the same word as in "the upward call of God.") What are the upward things we're supposed to set our minds on and seek? And what are the things on earth we're to avoid?

Paul goes on: "Therefore, consider the members of your earthly body as dead to immorality, impurity, passion, evil desire, and greed (which amounts to idolatry), anger, wrath, malice, slander, and abusive speech. Don't lie to one another." These are the things on earth. Then Paul writes about the upward things.

> And so, as those who've been chosen by God, holy and beloved, put on a heart of compassion, kindness, humility, gentleness, and patience, putting up with one another and forgiving each other. Whoever has a complaint against anyone, just as the Lord forgave you, so also should you. And beyond all these things, put on love, which is the perfect bond of unity. And let the peace of Christ rule in your hearts, to which indeed you were called in one body, and be thankful. Let the word of Christ dwell in you richly, with all wisdom teaching and admonishing one another with psalms and hymns and spiritual songs, singing with

> thankfulness in your hearts to God. And whatever
> you do in word or deed, do all in the name of the
> Lord Jesus, giving thanks through him to God the
> Father.

Here then are the upward things. The upward call of God
in Christ Jesus is a call to compassion, kindness, humility,
meekness, patience, putting up with one another, for-
giveness, love, peace, thanksgiving, being engrossed in
Christ's word, teaching each other, and urging each other
on in the Christian life. It's Christian music. It's serving
Christ whatever your occupation is. These are the things
we're called up to.

So "let's go fly a kite, up to the highest height, and send it
soaring up through the atmosphere, up where the air is
clear." Up where you who enter the world of business will
show more interest in charity than in amassing a private
fortune. Up where you who become medical doctors will
fan out into ghettos and small towns and rural areas and
countries of the two-thirds world instead of huddling
together on Easy Street in Vanity Fair. Up where you who
turn into scientists and technicians will carry on your
research and technology according to moral principles
rather than according to the desire to advance knowledge
for its own sake and do what's possible just because it *is*
possible. Up where you who enter various forms of
Christian ministry will serve the church in humility rather
than split the church by going out for personal popularity.
Up where you who become teachers will serve students,
not browbeat them. Up where you who get married will
live with your spouses for a lifetime. Up where all of us
can breathe the pure oxygen of God's Spirit. With our
lungs full of that—full of HIM—some bright day we'll
streak across the finish line in a blaze of glory, seize

the prize of eternal life, run a victory lap, sit down, and have another baccalaureate service.

Auf wiedersehen. See you then.

Godspeed

*~ Delivered at a retirement dinner for
philosophy professor Robert Wennberg ~*

Bob,

Instead of talking to others about you and letting you listen in, I'm going to talk to you and let them listen. Our provost assigned me the topic of your contributions to the ethos of Westmont. She apologized for the vagueness of ethos as a topic. "But how fitting!" I thought. "*Ethos* is a Greek word. It didn't even change spelling, pronunciation, or meaning when it came over into English. I used to teach Greek. You teach philosophy. Philosophy started with the Greeks. You specialize in ethics, and the word *ethics* comes from the word *ethos*. So everything about my assignment fits together perfectly."

What then have been your contributions to the ethos of Westmont? The natural place to begin is with retirement dinners like this one. The president of my seminary was so full of enthusiasm that people said he'd preach at his own funeral. This dinner isn't a funeral (though a certain sadness does lurk behind our levity), but you've made yourself so much a part of our retirement dinners that you've just now presented the slide show of your own career at the college. It's a wonder you aren't in charge of the whole affair. You *personify* the ethos of these dinners. It's tempting to say your humorous performances put you in league with the current crop of late night talk show hosts on television: Jay Leno and Dave Letterman, for instance. But that comparison would be too coarse. I prefer to compare you with the father of them all, Jack Paar. His savoir faire made his successors look like amateúrs. Your humor has displayed a similar savoir faire, as well it should in a college setting. (By the way, I said "amateúrs" to honor you with Sir John Gielgud's pronunciation in your favorite movie, "Chariots of Fire.")

Here's another contribution you've made to the ethos of Westmont, doubtless a more important one. We sometimes joke good-naturedly about your often saying, "I'm of two minds on that question." What you've seriously done, though, is to set us an example of seeing all sides of an issue; and by your example you've led us to do the same. You've taught us not only to see all sides. You've also taught us to appreciate the strength of arguments for positions that in the end we don't agree with, to respect their strength, and to nuance our own arguments and positions accordingly. In other words, you've played a major role in saving Westmont from obscurantism.

That thought brings me to what others in our midst have independently mentioned to me. It's a refusal to limit your efforts to teaching, research, and writing. You set for yourself a large vision of the college. You've involved yourself in its whole life. Not that obstacles didn't stand in the way. When a nominating committee put your name and Bud Blankenbaker's on the ballot for election to the Faculty Personnel Committee (as we now call it), an older member of the faculty objected from the floor of a business meeting that the two of you were untrustworthy and that therefore a third nominee was needed. But they couldn't find one. So they had to choose between you and Bud. They chose Bud, who—ironically—later became academic dean. Not to be deterred, though—and just as ironically, you became both associate academic dean at one point and vice-chair of the faculty no fewer than four times. You also served the college—you served *us*—on thirty-nine committees, task forces, and such like. Thirty-nine, like the apostle Paul's "forty stripes save one." And that number is probably incomplete, since you stopped updating your CV ten years ago, when you got full professorship, so that nowadays full professors have to join accountability groups—another of your contributions to our ethos. You're hardly a masochist; so you must have been the victim of a persecution inflicted by us who are sitting here trying to atone for the sins we committed against you by piling too many responsibilities on your back.

You spearheaded the establishing of Phi Kappa Phi as an honor society on our campus. You integrated your own field of philosophy with history, law, psychology, religion, biology, business, and medicine. You spoke on such matters to alumni and in the community of Santa Barbara. I was particularly intrigued by the title of one of your presentations for Westmont in the Village during the Fall of 1990. Your CV lists the topic as "Dessert Storm and the Morality of War." "Now that's my kind of war," I thought to myself on reading that entry. "I bet it meets Bob's criteria for a just war. The only question is which side should win, chocolate or vanilla." In any case, you've championed the liberal arts and modeled a willingness to serve the whole college outside as well as inside your field of specialty. And we're all the richer for it.

These contributions to the ethos of Westmont, and others that could be added, stem it seems to me from your remarkable generosity of spirit. It's this generosity that makes your humor playful and gentle rather than demeaning, that enables you to see and appreciate all sides of an issue, that propels both your interest in a wide variety of subjects and your willingness to serve the whole college in a wide variety of ways. Finally, your generosity of spirit endears you as an all-weather friend to your colleagues, a friend who has extended them a charity that "envieth not," "vaunteth not itself," "seeketh not her own," "is not easily provoked," and "rejoiceth in the truth." Thank you, Bob, for showing me such charity. Thanks from all of us.

Godspeed.

Christ as Creator

*~ Delivered at the memorial service for Lyle Hillegas,
former teacher at and president of Westmont College,
who before his death chose the topic ~*

For a number of years Lyle Hillegas and I taught together in the same department at Westmont College. So in memory of our sharing that role, I'm going to don the mantle of a teacher for a few minutes and deliver a homily that'll probably sound like a mini-lecture. Maybe you wouldn't mind playing the role of students, perhaps Lyle's students more than mine.

We all know how the Bible begins. It begins *at* the beginning *with* the beginning.

Genesis 1:1: "In the beginning God created the heavens and the earth." That's a plain enough statement, straightforward enough. But right away things get a little complicated, a little wrinkled, you might say, because the very next verse says that the earth was "without form and void," that "darkness was over the surface of the deep," and that "God's Spirit," like a wind, "was moving over the surface of the waters." What's this about God's Spirit? There was God. Now he has a Spirit, a Spirit that has something mysterious to do with creation.

If we make a giant leap to the New Testament, the story of creation gets another wrinkle. Take the first three verses of John's Gospel, for instance: "In the beginning [an echo of Genesis 1:1] was the Word." Despite the obvious echo of Genesis, there's no reference to God or to his having created everything—or anything, for that matter. As if to compensate for these omissions, though, John immediately states, "The Word was with God, and the Word was God."

Then John takes us back to the beginning and finally does say something about the creation: "This one [the Word] was in the beginning with God. All things came into existence through him [the Word], and apart from him there came into existence not even one thing that did come into existence."

Fair enough, but it takes John over a dozen more verses to tell us that this Word, God's agent in creation who himself was God though also distinguishable from God, rather like God's Spirit back in Genesis—it takes John over a dozen more verses to tell us that this Word appeared on earth, much later than the creation, in the person and flesh of Jesus Christ or, to use John's picturesque phrase, that the Word "tabernacled among us"—an allusion to the Old Testament tabernacle, a portable tent in which God as Spirit dwelt among his people Israel. Only here it's God as the Word-made-*flesh* that dwelt among us.

The apostle Paul puts it a lot more succinctly: "For all things in heaven and on earth, visible and invisible . . . were created in him ['God's beloved Son']. [Which is to say that] all things exist as created through him and for him" (Colossians 1:16). So as God the Father's agent in creation, the preincarnate Christ was the Creator of all that exists.

Christ's functioning as Creator had everything to do with the dim and distant past, the beginning. But what does it have to do with us, or with the death of Lyle Hillegas? For an answer, let's go back to the apostle Paul, this time to his second letter to the Christians in Corinth: "If anyone is in Christ, that person is a new creation. The old things have passed away. Look! New things have come into existence!" (5:17). You come to be "in Christ" by believing in him. Then you receive God's Spirit, the very Spirit that blew over the chaotic waters at the old creation. But he's also the Spirit who indwells Christ, God's Son.

So if you have the Spirit who indwells Christ, you too are in Christ.

But why a new creation in him? Answer: Because God raised him from the dead, Jesus Christ is himself the beginning of a new creation, so that anyone who is in him by faith helps make up this new creation. Such a person becomes a new creation in miniature within the new creation at large that Jesus embodies. The old things that have passed away are the sinful behaviors that characterized us as fallen creatures before incorporation into Christ. The new things that have come into existence are the godly behaviors that characterize us if we've truly been created anew in him.

And here's the payoff. The passing away of those old things and the coming into existence of these new things, this new creation consisting of individual believers in Christ merely previews—I should say, *gloriously* previews—what John the seer records on a grand scale in Revelation 21:1–6:

> And I saw a new heaven and a new earth, for the first heaven and the first earth had passed away. And the sea [those threatening, storm-tossed waters of the old creation] doesn't exist any more. And I saw the holy city, the New Jerusalem, descending out of heaven from God, prepared as a bride adorned for her husband.
>
> And I heard a loud voice from the throne, saying, "Look! The tabernacle of God is with human beings. And he'll tabernacle with them. And they'll be his peoples, and God himself will be with them. And he'll wipe away every tear out of their eyes, and there won't be death any more. Neither will there be grief or crying or pain any more, because

the first things have passed away." And the one sitting on the throne said, "Look! I'm making all things new!" And he says, "Write [what you've just heard], because these words are faithful and true." And he said to me, "They've come into existence! [The new heaven and the new earth are so sure to come into existence that they might as well have already done so.] I am the Alpha and the Omega, the Beginning and the End. To the person who's thirsting I'll give as a gift [water] from the spring of the water of life."

Christ as Creator in the beginning! Christ as Creator at the end! As such, he personifies the beginning. He personifies the end. But the end is only a beginning, the beginning of everlasting life in a new, resurrected body, part and parcel of the new creation previewed right now in every Christian conversion, and previewed just recently and gracefully in the Christian life of our dear departed friend.

So this little Scripture lesson closes with an invitation that goes out to all, to all of you, who long for new life in Christ. As the Creator of that life he issues this invitation, nearly the last verse in the Bible: "Let the person who wishes take as a gift the water of life" (Revelation 22:17).

Addendum

Some Remarks on "The Seventh Seal" by Ingmar Bergman

~ Delivered after the showing of a film ~

Ingmar Bergman is a Swedish cinematographer whose work belongs to what is called "the serious cinema." Ordinarily he writes his own screenplays and directs the filming of them. The title of this particular film, "The Seventh Seal," comes from the book of Revelation in the Bible and thus sets an apocalyptic tone to give a feeling that the film deals with ultimate issues, such as the ultimate reality for human beings, the actual or possible significance of human action, the meaningfulness or unmeaningfulness of religion, and the dilemma of modern people.

In viewing the film we immediately notice that for Bergman the ultimate reality about human existence is death. The film begins and ends with death. The carrion-feeding vulture ominously circles in the sky at both beginning and end. One of the opening scenes features a horrid death-head. The closing scene features the dance of death. A chess game with the angel of death continues throughout the film. Death shows itself in many other ways as well. In other words, life is one long game to defeat death, but death always wins. This preoccupation with death, with the threat of nonexistence, with the fact that death haunts life, points up one of the existential aspects of Bergman's philosophy.

To come closer to the meaning of the film we should determine what kinds of people the main characters represent. The squire represents a sensual person. The naughty little ditty he sings toward the beginning of the film isn't a signal that you're about to see a sexy movie. Just the opposite, in fact. It's to tell you that the squire is a sensual man, so that when he later says to the girl whom he saves from death and refuses to rape, "I've wearied of that kind of love," you know that *he* knows what he's talking about. Bergman has turned preacher at this point. He's saying that the contemporary notion that sexual play brings meaning and fulfillment in life is a myth which needs to be demythologized. Sex is highly over-rated. The squire has tried it and failed. That same lesson is to be learned from the actor who was seduced and later cut down by death as he sought safety on the limb of a tree. Only, the actor was an ignorant fool being led to the slaughter like a dumb animal, whereas the squire is a worldly wise man whose failure to find satisfaction in sensuality has bred cynicism. Though a man of action who does what he knows must be done, he does it with a cynical attitude.

As Christians we agree with Bergman that sensuality turns out to be meaningless. But this seems to be *all* that Bergman has to say. We have to add that sensuality isn't only meaningless, it's also wrong. It's wrong because it violates the holy laws of God, which are rooted in his very nature. But of course Bergman cannot say so, because for him there is no such God.

Antonius Block is a refined, sophisticated modern man. He's disillusioned with organized religion (represented by the witch hunt) and with traditional causes (represented by the crusades). He has lost his faith. But he's intelligent and sincere. He desires authenticity. He can't stand sham and pretence. He values honesty above all. He wants to believe, but he can't. There are too many intellectual problems. Yet he's facing death, he's facing certain nonexistence. He desperately tries to find *some* meaning, *some* significance in life before he dies. Time is running out. He must do something truly worthwhile *now*. The crusades have proved a total loss so far as he is concerned. How can he possibly salvage some significance for his life?

On the other hand, we see the clown and his family. They're reminiscent of the holy family—Joseph, Mary, and the infant. But beyond that reminiscence, the clown represents the truly pious person. He has simple, open-hearted faith. He sees visions that others scoff at, but he knows they're real. At least to *him* they are. Bergman has nothing but scorn for the professional religionists, but portrays the clown sympathetically, even enviously. But to Bergman this true piety of the clown is nonrational, visionary, mystical. Bergman here reveals his view—a very common view nowadays—that the only valid type of religion consists in the new mysticism. For to him religion can't be truly rational.

The clown also represents a persecuted Christian. Recall the inn scene where he's badgered, mocked, and barely escapes with his life. He's also a happy Christian. Recall the idyllic family scenes bathed in sunlight. He escapes death. He lives forever, or at least has hope, symbolized by the infant son who will "carry on" (compare the rising sun in the last scene). Bergman himself has said that each of his films ends with the possibility of hope. The rising sun and new day of the last scene doubtless represent this possibility of hope. But two things must be said about it: (1) The hope is entirely nonrational and mystical, a circumstance that leaves modern people in the dilemma that to believe they must sacrifice their intellects, something impossible to do and remain fully honest. (2) The setting of the new day is back on the beach where the film started. You're supposed to infer that the chess game with death is going to be played all over again, the cycle repeating itself with cruel monotony.

As a thoroughly modern man, Bergman himself is Block. But he wishes he could be the clown. He wishes he could believe, but thinks his intelligence and knowledge as a modern, post-crusades man denies him the luxury of faith if he's to remain true to himself. But here we must disagree somewhat with Bergman. Antonius Block is a little *too* honest in his intellectual doubts to be a realistic figure. Most of us have to struggle to be honest, at least completely so. But not Block, and therefore he isn't a wholly believable figure.

To be sure, people do have intellectual difficulties. But such difficulties aren't peculiar to moderns. People have always had intellectual problems with the Christian faith. The apostle Thomas did. So did the Athenians who heard Paul preach. There was widespread disbelief in the Graeco-Roman pantheon at the very time Christianity arose and spread. Bergman fails to point out that intellectual problems are all mixed up with moral problems, that faith demands commitment, obedience, rectitude, and a cutting down of human pride and pretensions of merit. As a result it is probably impossible to disentangle genuine intellectual problems from the perversity of those who claim they can't believe. Part (not all) of their problem is that they *will* not believe. Bergman has been too simplistic in portraying Block. Bergman underestimates human depravity, doubtless because he is portraying himself; and all of us are blind to our own dishonesties, though very keen-sighted in pointing out the dishonesties of others.

Does Block succeed in performing one significant act before death takes him? Yes. When he knocks some pieces off the chess board, death thinks that Block is trying to gain a fresh start in the game. But Block has tricked death by engrossing the attention of death on the chessboard, so that the clown and his family are able to escape. This trick constitutes the single significant act of Block, the one act that gives meaning to his life in the face of death. And so, since for Bergman there is no God to love anymore, love for neighbor becomes the first commandment instead of the second. As the clown and his family flee through the forest during the midnight storm, the wife asks her husband what is happening. The clown answers that the storm is passing over them. His answer alludes to the Passover story in the book of Exodus, where the angel of death (symbolized by the storm in the film) passed over the houses of the Israelites, God's people, but took the firstborn of the Egyptians.

But even that incident doesn't provide very great encouragement. In the castle scene toward the end, the girl who followed the squire to become his wife says, "It is finished." The statement is, of course, borrowed from one of the last words of Christ from the cross. In Bergman, however, it means, "This is the end; there is no more." It's a cry of despair, or of brave resignation, or perhaps of relieved acceptance of death as an escape from the horrors of life. In any case, the meaning is far different from the biblical connotation of the statement. On the lips of the dying Jesus, "It is finished!" means not only, "Death has come; I'm about to die," but also, "It is accomplished! The work of redemption is done!" It's a cry of victory in death, even through and by means of death. For out of Christ's death comes eternal life. Here lies a big difference between the gospel and humanism.

Our task as Christians is to show that believing in Jesus can be intelligent and truly pious and open-hearted at the same time. But we must take care not to lose the simplicity of faith in our attempt to make it intellectually respectable. If we do lose that simplicity, Bergman and those like him will not be attracted to it anymore.

Printed in Great Britain
by Amazon